17 BIG BETS
FOR A
BETTER
WORLD

Manon Otto
snoscapes@gmail.com

Stig Tackmann
Kristian Kampmann
Henrik Skovby

17 BIG BETS
FOR A
BETTER
WORLD

Historika

Published by Forlaget Historika / Gad Publishers A/S, 2016
Gad Publishers A/S, Fiolstræde 31, 1171 København K, Denmark
www.gad.dk

Grateful acknowledgement to Danida (Danish Development Agency) and
Danidas Oplysningsbevilling for contributing to this book

Grateful acknowledgement is made for permission to use and reprint the following images:
Page 14: © GPE/Grant Ellis; Page 20-21: © Feed My Starving Children (FMSC), FMSC
Distribution Partner – Haiti, Flickr, with Creative Commons Attribution 2.0 Generic /
desaturated from original; Page 24: Picture first from the top: © Mr. Naman Bhojani; Page
31: © Mike Debelak; Page 34: © Mark Ostow; Page 42: © Thomas Delhemmes; Page 46:
Picture first from the top: © Rose Studios LLC; Page 58: © OECD/Herve Cortinat; Page 68: ©
CERN, Christian Beutler; Page 74-75: © CERN, Max Brice; Page 85: © Basil D Soufi, Creative
Commons Attribution-Share Alike 3.0 Unported license / desaturated from original; Page
88: © Andy Cantillon; Page 102: © Acumen; Page 108-109: © Mike Debelak; Page 112: ©
Kailash Satyarthi Children's Foundation; Page 120-121: © Bijay chaurasia, Creative Commons
Attribution-Share Alike 4.0 International license / desaturated from original; Page 124: © Inter-
American Development Bank: IDB; Page 128-129: © Feed My Starving Children (FMSC), FMSC
Distribution Partner – Haiti, Flickr, with Creative Commons / desaturated from original; Page
132: Picture first from the top: © Erin Lubin/Greenpeace. Picture second from the top: © Alex
Yallop/Greenpeace; Page 140-141: © Shayne Robinson/Greenpeace; Page 144: © Courtesy of
Equity Bank; Page 154: © 2016 Robert Houser; Page 166: © Romero & Romero Photography;
Page 174-175: © Petri Allekotte; Page 178: © Federal Ministry of Environment, Nigeria; Page
185: © Gerd Altmann; Page 188: © Olafur Eliasson, Anders Sune Berg, 2016; Page 194-195: ©
2015 Olafur Eliasson Ice Watch by Olafur Eliasson and Minik Rosing, Place du Panthéon, Paris,
2015. Photo: Martin Argyroglo

Printed in Lithuania by Clemenstrykkeriet

Library of Congress Cataloging-in-Publication Data is on file with the Library of Congress
ISBN 978-87-93229-54-9

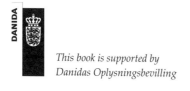

This book is supported by
Danidas Oplysningsbevilling

Special thanks to

Jill Freebury, Hans Uldall-Poulsen, Kasper Bjerre/Salvador, and Morten Nyegaard for all the ongoing help on proofreading, data visualization and design.

Also, this book has only been possible due to the relentless effort of: Nelson Muffuh (UNFPA) and Joe Colombano (Post-2015 Development Planning Unit, United Nations); Mark Suzman and Anugraha Palan (Bill & Melinda Gates Foundation); Stephen Browne (Future United Nations Development System) Emily Ross (United Nations Foundation); Abdul Hannan (UN); Rebecca Eastmond (JP Morgan); Michael Zhao.

From Dalberg, a very special thanks to: James Mwangi, Varad Pande, Edwin Macharia, Joe Dougherty, Yana Kakar, Aly-Khan Jamal, Rajen Makhijani, Devang Vussonji, Pritha Venkatachalam, Matt Frazier, Serena Guarnaschelli, Sonila Cook, Oren Ahoobim, Paul Callan, Ciku Kimeria, and CJ Fonzi.

Contents

Foreword

The 2030 Agenda and 17 Global Goals for Sustainable Development were adopted by all member states at the United Nations General Assembly last year. For the first time in history, we now have a broad global ambition and framework to make our world a more peaceful, inclusive, and sustainable one – for this generation and for those to come.

To achieve the new Global Goals, new partnerships and new resources are needed. We must think and act outside the box.

In this book, thought leaders provide their big bets on a better world. Published early on in the life of the Global Goals, this publication can inspire states, civil society, the private sector, and citizens at large to think outside the box on implementation.

This book presents 17 bold and innovative solutions. From the Global Partnership for Education, to one of East Africa's leading banks and to the busy kitchen of Michelin chef Dan Barber, this book offers many fresh perspectives. I hope its publication begins a dialogue on how we can identify and get behind the most promising big bets.

Helen Clark,
Administrator of the United
Nations Development Programme and former
Prime Minister of New Zealand.

Introduction

Why the world urgently needs Big Bets

History is driven by great inventions of astonishing impact. Faced with harsh conditions and intractable challenges, humans have always been capable of coming up with new solutions to improve their lives and chances for survival. Smallpox vaccine, the Green Revolution, and the mesmerizing anti-poverty movement of the last two decades are just a few examples of real transformational ideas that have brought about real change.

2015 was a landmark year for global development. It marked the successful termination of the Millennium Development Goals (MDG) and the adoption of the Global Goals on sustainable development. The Global Goals, the most ambitious project the international community has ever agreed on, consists of 17 goals and 169 targets, ranging from the pursuit of gender equality and quality education to climate action and promotion of inclusive societies.

While the MDGs took the global development agenda a

long way – lifting more than 1 billion people out of poverty, increasing primary school enrollment and providing electricity to almost 2 billion people – the Global Goals set out to finish the job. The Global Goals apply to all. They cut across geographies, ethnicities and political orientations and they entail a shared responsibility to make the world a better place for everybody.

As the global community embarks on its path toward implementing the Global Goals on sustainable development, innovation and disruptive thinking is once again our best chance of addressing the world's most pressing issues. Close to a billion people still live in poverty, the earth is getting warmer every month that passes, and armed conflict is on the rise in many places. The clock is ticking and with the new goals, we have given ourselves an ambitious timeline. In 15 years, we – the global community – need to successfully implement and realize the vision for sustainable development.

The world stands at a crossroads, and the coming years will set the trend for future generations. As UN Secretary General Ban-Ki Moon has phrased it: *"We are the first generation that can end poverty, and the last one that can take steps to avoid the worst impacts of climate change.[1]"* Right now, we have a window of opportunity to deliver. In the wake of what might be the largest and most inclusive consultation process in our world's history, the international community is committed to agree on the most holistic path towards a sustainable future. The question is: how do we deliver?

This book is based on a simple argument: to reach the Global Goals in 15 years, innovation is a necessity. If we are to end poverty and ensure prosperity for all, we must abandon silo thinking and channel our resources towards the very best ideas. To reach the Global Goals, we need academics, artists, bureaucrats, entrepreneurs, investors, and many more to join forces and galvanize around the transformations that can bring us over the finish line as quickly as possible. In short, there is an urgent need to make big bets.

What is our collective challenge?

Despite the impressive progress over the past 15 years, we are still facing enormous hurdles. To give a more concrete sense of the type of challenges that we are facing, here are some of the most dire planetary facts:

- More than 800 million people still live in extreme poverty
- 783 million people do not have access to clean water
- Almost 2.5 billion people do not have access to adequate sanitation
- In 2014, an average 42,500 people became refugees, asylum seekers, or were internally displaced every day
- Inequality is staggering as just 62 people own the same wealth as half the world
- Only four in ten young women and men aged 15–24 were employed in 2015
- Global emissions of carbon dioxide have increased by over 50% since 1990
- And 57 million children of primary school age are out of school[2]

On the funding side, similar challenges exist. To achieve the Global Goals, an estimated annual investment of US$ 3,900 billion is needed[3]. This corresponds to the combined GNP of India and Brazil in 2015[4]. Based on the current levels of public and private investments in development, this leaves an annual investment gap of US$ 2,500 billion – 18 times more than the current level of official development assistance from donor governments. To bridge the funding gap, private investments need to be quadrupled. In education alone, an estimated US$ 250 billion is needed to invest in schools, infrastructure and material – per year[5].

What is a big bet?

So what is a big bet? Big bets are the chances we take to breed transformative shifts; the creative ideas with which we push our thinking; the investments made in solutions to current and future challenges. A big bet might be unrealistic or naïve, but it helps us expand our potential range of solutions. Ultimately, big bets are what cause progress and change - even when challenges seem insurmountable.

Throughout history, innovations and creative thinking have managed to leap-frog global development and lift people out of poverty. When Edward Jenner introduced smallpox vaccine in 1796, his results were met with fierce skepticism. The vaccine was claimed to be ungodly and critics ridiculed him. As the remarkable results of the vaccination won out, the vaccine was adopted and millions of lives have been saved from a range of once terrifying diseases. In this way, a simple innovative idea – to insert pus, taken from a cowpox, into the arm of a boy to avoid smallpox – became one of the biggest contributions to human development throughout history. Whether we speak of Norman Borlaug's Green Revolution, Nikola Tesla's invention of alternating current or Tim-Berner

Lee's development of the World Wide Web – transformative ideas have been vital in driving human development forward.

In this book, 17 global thought leaders present their big bet for a better world. The task has been straightforward: what idea, innovation or thought would you encourage the world community to adopt to maximize the chances that we reach the Global Goals by 2030?

The answers have been remarkable and resulted in this anthology. Each contribution represents a concrete bet for a better world and the book in its entirety thus represents a catalog of ideas aimed at accelerating the implementation of the Global Goals. It is our hope that these perspective and thoughts will help pave the way towards a better world.

Stig Tackmann, Editor-in-Chief, Dalberg
Henrik Skovby, Chairman, Dalberg

---

1. www.un.org/press/en/2015/sgsm16800.doc.htm
2. OECD, 2015; UNWater.org, 2013; UNHCR, 2014; Oxfam, An Economy for the 1%, 2016; Un.org: http://www.un.org/millenniumgoals/poverty.shtml; MDG Progress Report, 2015
3. UNCTAD, Global Investment report 2014
4. IMF, World Economic Outlook, April 2016
5. UNCTAD, Global Investment report 2014

Can the Appearance Industry Do a Makeover of Girls' Education?

By **Julia Gillard**

Julia Gillard was Australia's 27th Prime Minister between 2010 and 2013. She is now the Board Chair of the Global Partnership for Education and a Senior Distinguished Fellow at the Center for Universal Education at Brookings. Before becoming Prime Minister, Ms. Gillard was Deputy Prime Minister and Minister for Education, Employment and Workplace Relations and Social Inclusion. Prior to entering politics, Ms. Gillard worked as a solicitor in Melbourne with the law firm Slater and Gordon and became a Partner in 1990. Ms. Gillard retired from political life following the 2013 Australian national election.

Julia Gillard focuses on the appearance industry. The big bet is to enable this growing sector to use its strength as a force for good by becoming a major funder of girls' education in the poorest parts of the world. Adding a small voluntary levy on fashion products as donations to girls' education would not deter purchasers. Rather, it would be an enormous step towards gender parity in education. Making sure that all girls receive a quality education is not only a fundamental right but also the most effective way of bringing about positive change.

Australians love to travel. Last year, the population of just 23 million people took more than nine million trips overseas. Given our geographic position in the world, traveling Australians quickly become aficionados of major hub airports. Singapore, Dubai, Hong Kong, Doha – seasoned Australian travelers can spend hours discussing which is best.

However, while fine distinctions can be made, every major international airport has a similar look and feel. Every one is a gleaming citadel of shopping with the allure of duty free electronics, liquor and, for those determined to do themselves harm, cigarettes. Each has acres allocated to the beauty and high fashion industries – the appearance industry – and its lotions, potions, perfumes and branded clothing and accessories.

Of course, there is no need to be wheeling carry-on luggage to see the appearance industry on display. The ground floor of any major department store flaunts the same beauty elixirs, and around the world, major shopping centers are home to stores dedicated to brands which are synonymous with luxury.

The appeal of the counters and stores is just one aspect of the marketing genius displayed by the appearance industry. Over decades, glamor, sex appeal, and pseudo-science have all been employed to persuade women that they just cannot live without that cream, that hand bag, that brand on their clothing.

Yet, all the billions of dollars spent by the appearance industry on promotion have not left it unblemished or scandal-free. Witness the backlash that has been associated with the use of under-age and under-weight models, the successful campaigning that has occurred against animals being used in testing and the growing recognition of the environmental problems caused by micro-beads. The appearance industry continues to weather social media-fueled storms.

But overall, its image in the eyes of consumers is positive. Indeed, the appearance industry is dynamic, valuable and growing. Industry estimates are that the hair care, cosmetics, skin care and fragrance industry will hit a global value of US$ 265 billion by 2017. Growth rates in the premium end of the market are running at almost 5%[1].

The fashion industry has been discussed in United States Congress Joint Economic Committee documents and is estimated to be worth US$ 1.2 trillion globally per annum[2]. Some estimates range as high as US$ 1.7 trillion. Clearly, the luxury fashion market is one component of these broad industry valuations and defining and quantifying it is not an easy task. However, the fact that Vuitton, Gucci, Hermes, Coach, Cartier, Prada, Chanel and Burberry all appear in the Forbes top 100 companies list gives a sense of the dimensions of the luxury market.

So my big idea is to enable the appearance industry to use its strength as a force for good by having it become a major funder of girls' education in the poorest parts of the world.

Why pick this industry? And why girls' education?

First, because it is an industry which predominantly focuses on sales to women. Supporting girls' education is a natural fit.

Second, because it is an industry where image and reality blur into one. In any major international airport or luxury shopping center, you can buy a scarf worth US$ 1,825, a handbag worth US$ 5,750, a 20-milliliter (0.68-oz.) jar of eye cream worth US$ 380 or 14.79-milliliter (0.5-oz.) bottle of perfume for US$ 200. Have some fun, try to guess the brands of these items. They are all well known. None of these items costs anything like their sale price to produce. What's selling is the image and promise associated with the brand.

That means in the appearance industry, campaigns that affect perceptions can have a real impact. It also means that demand is inelastic, meaning it is not sensitive to increases in price. For the kinds of goods whose prices are disclosed above, it is fanciful to imagine that adding a levy of up to 5% for donations to girls' education would deter purchasers. Indeed, according to the US Bureau of Statistics, the price of luxury goods has risen 60% over the last decade and economic research about luxury branding shows higher prices fuel perceptions of exclusivity which pique demand rather than suppress it.

Third, because the appearance industry is an eco-system. The fashion industry gives birth to supermodels, who become so iconic that their endorsement or repudiation can make or break a product. The film industry gives us accomplished and beautiful actresses who become brand endorsers or creators of their own perfumes and clothing lines. The fashion magazines skillfully seek to hold our attention on the articles and the advertisements featuring supermodels, actresses, and other celebrities woven into both. A campaign for girls' education can appeal to many players in this ecosystem and therefore change the whole of the environment.

At the beginning, the girls' education levy could be small, but the idea could spread rapidly. The ground is fertile, with some brands already associating with philanthropic causes.

Imagine this: a supermodel and two female global celebrities announce that all the appearance industry products produced in their name or with their endorsement will initially have a girls' education levy of 1%, which will rise over time to 3%. One of the major integrated beauty and fashion brands which sell clothes, shoes, handbags, perfume, and cosmetics makes the same announcement. A major fashion magazine joins the campaigning, saying it will publish each month a list of products its readers can buy which have the levy in place.

Social media snowballs the campaign, and quite quickly it becomes a competitive disadvantage for consumers for a product to be levy-free. Suddenly, support for girls' education has a sizeable and growing revenue stream. No government regulation would need to be involved. Rather, the levy would emerge as an industry standard because of the preferences of purchasers and the social awareness of those in the appearance industry.

Imagine how the relevance of the global appearance industry would increase if the industry not only focused on making young girls look smart but also on actually being smart.

Where would the funds go? It would be vital for the credibility of this levy that the money raised went to organizations that have the ability to make a real difference to girls' education. The Global Partnership for Education stands out as the only multilateral organization solely dedicated to education. There are a number of high-quality non-government organizations, including Camfed (the Campaign for Female Education), which have a strong track record in supporting girls' education. UNICEF also does wonderful work and already benefits from purchases of a specially designed Vuitton pendant and bracelet.

However, the larger question is why should girls' education be the target of the funds? The answer put simply, is because investing in girls' educations is the most effective way of causing a change in our world. An educated girl is less likely to be forced into early marriage or to contract HIV/AIDS. An educated woman is likely to choose to have fewer children than an uneducated woman and the children of educated women are more likely to survive infant-hood, be vaccinated and become educated themselves. The earnings of an educated woman are far more likely to be invested in her family's support than the earnings of a man. The impact of educating a girl flows across generations and changes the ability of families and communities to move out of poverty. There is a reason that terrorists target the education of girls. They fear such a powerful agent of change.

While the advantages of educating girls are clear, progress towards gender parity in accessing high-quality school education is too slow. Indeed, at current rates of change it will not be until 2111 that the world sees the first generation of sub-Saharan African girls who have universally accessed primary and lower secondary school. The poorest girls will get access a full seventy years after the most advantaged boys. We know how to change this time-line, to accelerate access to school for girls. What we lack is the resources to do so.

The appearance industry wants to sell us all a dream. An enticing but unattainable dream of physical perfection and agelessness. My big idea is that the dream we buy from the appearance industry is one that is actually realizable. A dream of a world in which every girl gets access to the transformative power of education.

---

1. Michelle Yeomans. Global beauty market to reach US$ 265 billion in 2017 due to an increase in GDP. http://www.cosmeticsdesign.com

2. United States Congress Joint Economic Committee. The Economic Impact of the Fashion Industry. February 2015. https://maloney.house.gov

A Unique Digital Identity for All

By **Nandan Nilekani** *&* **Varad Pande**

Nandan Nilekani was the founding Chairman of India's Unique Identification Authority of India, and took Aadhaar from drawing board to at-scale implementation. He continues to advise institutions and startups on many of the innovative applications of Aadhaar.

Varad Pande, Partner and Co-Lead of Financial Inclusion at Dalberg, was Special Advisor to India's Minister for Rural Development between 2009-14, a member of the team that launched Aadhaar.

Nandan Nilekani and Varad Pande present a clear big bet: to provide every individual with a digital identity capable of validating who they are. A digital identity not only has the potential to guarantee access to basic social services for all, but also to function as a platform for inclusion, innovation and the fight against corruption. This system has the potential to be adopted across the world, and the good news is that such a system is not just theory. In India today, almost a billion people are already beginning to benefit from such a digital identity system.

Seventy-year old Basudeb Pahan lives in a densely forested, remote area of Jharkhand, India. In order to receive his old-age pension of 400 rupees (US$ 6) a month, Pahan had to journey fifteen kilometers through hills and jungles to reach Ramgarh, the nearest settlement with a bank branch, where he would spend hours standing in line and pleading with government officials. He would typically end up spending ~10-15% of his pension in attempts to get his pension even before he received it. Pahan, the local government, and indeed the entire pension disbursement system were stuck in a time warp.

Then, in 2011, Pahan found himself transported from a dusty backwater of history into the forefront of India's technological revolution. Having enrolled in Aadhaar, India's biometric-backed unique digital identity program, for his next pension payment he walked just a few feet to the local village government office. There, a bank-appointed business correspondent entered Pahan's twelve-digit Aadhaar number into a device called a microATM. Pahan pressed his fingers on an attached fingerprint reader, and seconds later, the business correspondent was handing Pahan his money. Aadhaar had not only given him his first undeniable proof of identity but also transformed his experience as a citizen[1].

Buried in the Christmas tree of multiple Global Goals is target 16.9, which says: "by 2030 provide legal identity for all including birth registration." This is critical, but our experience over the last six years has convinced us that there is something even more fundamental, a unique digital identity. A digital identity system is just a way of validating that "you are whom you claim to be." The qualification requirements for such a system require a simple design, so it becomes an instrument of inclusion not exclusion. More complex ID systems, which require additional layers of validation, like a citizens' register, can be built as apps on a digital ID.

We believe that if done correctly – as an online, real-time, multi-modal biometric-based system with ubiquitous verifiability – digital identification has the potential to transform the life of every human being. In India today, almost a billion people, a sixth of humanity, are already beginning to benefit from such a system.

Why Digital Identity? An enabler of inclusion

For the voiceless millions, a digital proof of identity that is recognized by the 'system' in which the odds are stacked against you, is in itself empowering. In India, there are instances of people keeping their Aadhaar cards under lock and key to keep it safe – even though the card itself is not required for validation (your Aadhaar number and your biometric is all you need).

However, the benefits of a unique digital identity go far beyond just identity. India's Aadhaar system provides for e-KYC[2], where a person can share her Aadhaar data with accredited service providers like banks and mobile phone operators to facilitate opening an account. Its real-time authentication service allows for validation at the point of transaction, for example when Pahan walks in to get his pension.

In this way, a digital identity allows the poor and the marginalized to start off on a journey every human being should be entitled to – being able to prove who she is, whenever she wants to prove it – so she can open a bank account, get a mobile phone connection, book a train ticket, avail of a government service, etc.

Rebooting service delivery

If linked with a country's welfare system, a digital ID system can 'fix the leaky pipe of service delivery' that is the burden of every developing country. This has huge benefits for both citizens and the government.

For the citizen, the benefits are enormous. Because bio- metric data is unique, it can be used to eliminate both 'duplicates' (a person getting benefits multiple times) and 'fakes' (benefits being taken in the name of a non-existent or fictitious person) so that only the rightly entitled person gets the benefit or service. Because it allows for direct payments (using a system called the Aadhaar Payments Bridge) to the individual's account, and cash-out using biometric authentication at the last mile (using a system called Aadhaar Enabled Payment System), Aadhaar reduces the dependency of citizens on the web of intermediaries who traditionally enjoyed enormous discretion, thereby reducing hassle and corruption in the process. Because the ID is held in the cloud, the citizen can go to any accredited agent to do the transaction. This portability of benefits empowers the citizen and reduces the bargaining power of the supplier, the bane of the public delivery systems. The portability also ensures that if a person migrates to another location (something which is endemic in developing countries), his benefits travel with him.

The promise of Aadhaar to the citizen in service delivery is simple but powerful: the money or benefit should reach the right person, on time, in the full amount, and at her doorstep.

For the government, the gains are multifarious. It is not only more successful in reaching the intended target population, but it is also able to reduce its fiscal leakages, enabled by better targeting. In India for example, linking just the cooking gas (LPG) subsidy to an Aadhaar-linked delivery system has already enabled the government to save US$ 2.5 billion annually. It is estimated that through better targeting of benefits enabled by Aadhaar, India could save up to US$ 50 billion, or 1.2% of its Gross Domestic Product annually – an amount that can, for example, allow India to double its expenditure on public health, a crying national priority. An Aadhaar-based government delivery system also allows the government to have complete transparency of its fund's flow, knowing exactly where in its delivery chain the funds are sitting.

A platform for private sector innovation

The success of the Internet is often credited to the US Department of Defense, which made the initial investments in its creation. We all know about the innovation it enabled and how quickly it scaled. A digital ID system has similar potential. If structured in the right way, a Unique ID system can become a nucleus to spur innovation across the country. Much like the Internet, Aadhaar is crafted in what some people have called an "hourglass architecture", where minimal standardization at the "waist" of a layered architecture (in this case the Aadhaar platform) enables burgeoning innovation above (e.g., applications that build on it) and below (e.g., smartphones with built-in iris scanners that can do online authentication of Aadhaar, which is now available).

This is not a pipe dream; it has already begun in India. The financial services space is a good example. An initiative called the Unified Payment Interface (UPI), which builds on the Aadhaar system and will likely go live in 2016, is going to allow complete interoperability between different payment instruments like bank accounts and mobile wallets, unleashing seamless peer-to-peer payments among businesses and citizens. The system, being built by India's National Payments Corporation of India (NPCI), follows a host of payment system innovations that the NPCI has created over the last few years that include 'IMPS' (Immediate Payment Service) which allows for instant account-to-account payments. The open APIs of the UPI system will allow developers to create payment applications that build on Aadhaar. UPI is enabling a number of "financial addresses", including Aadhaar, which can be used for payment transactions.

We believe that if done right – as an online, real-time, multi-modal biometric-based system with ubiquitous verifiability – digital identification has the potential to transform the life of every human being.

Think of what this is going to enable: it will empower a billion Indians to transact digitally, with just their Aadhaar numbers, their biometrics and smartphones. What's more, the "digital exhaust", or digital data trails, that these transactions will create will be available to develop financial histories of individuals. These histories, which currently don't exist for the underbanked, open the door for the provision of credit products to a billion Indians and a 100 million micro-enterprises that are currently starved of institutional credit.

In India's case, the Aadhaar system has already "paid for itself" through just the savings in the government programs that now use it. The broader benefits to the economy, like the ones described above, make the return on investment monumental. Though the math still needs to be done, it is hard to imagine another public infrastructure investment with such enormous bang for the buck.

Is this achievable and scalable?

The confluence of four trends – near-universal mobile phone penetration, the maturing of biometric technology, decreasing the price of smartphones and the exponential increases in cheap computing power and storage – today make it feasible for a digital ID system and its benefits to become a reality. The scale of India's Aadhaar shows this is not just theory. The system and its applications have been thoroughly tested and debugged in India. The system is ready for rapid replication.

As the story of Pahan and so many others shows, a unique digital identity provides the promise of silently transforming what has been called a "flailing state", enabling us to leapfrog to a cutting-edge delivery system. It has the potential to be the world's largest service delivery, anti-corruption, inclusion and innovation platforms all at once. At a time when there is growing skepticism about the ability of governments to deliver, it has the potential of redeeming the social compact between government and citizens.

If the world is indeed serious about a new framework for sustainable development – one that guarantees every human being access to basic social services, as well as a chance to climb the ladder of opportunity and empowerment – then a unique digital identity has to be the foundational building block.

---

1. The anecdote is adapted from the book 'Rebooting India: Realizing a billion aspirations', by Nandan Nilekani and Viral Shah
2. e-KYC is an solution to complete the Know Your Customer process electronically with direct authorization by the resident. The core idea of the e-KYC Aadhaar service is to enable individuals to authorise service providers to receive electronic copy of their proof of identity and address.

A Menu for 2030

By **Dan Barber**

Dan Barber is the Chef of Blue Hill, a restaurant in Manhattan's West Village, and Blue Hill at Stone Barns, located within the nonprofit farm and education center, Stone Barns Center for Food & Agriculture. In his New York Times bestselling book, The Third Plate: Field Notes on the Future of Food, Barber explores how we can reshape our ways of eating and farming to maximize the health of the land.

The conventional food system cannot be sustained. The way we eat and farm harms human health and erodes natural resources. As such, we have to reimagine our diets for the future. Dan Barber asks a difficult question: what kind of menu will move us closer to achieving the Global Goals in 2030? Answering this question, Barber outlines a four course menu that not only sustains the world, but also has the potential to spark improvements for people and planet.

We need radical thinking, but we don't need a revolution. In order to feed the world sustainably, we need to reimagine the way we eat.

Each day, we see more irrefutable evidence that our global food system is broken. Eroding soils, falling water tables for irrigation, collapsing fisheries, shrinking forests, and diminishing biodiversity represent only a handful of the environmental problems wrought by our food system – problems that will continue to multiply with, and contribute to, global warming.

Our health has suffered, too. Rising rates of food-borne illnesses, malnutrition and diet-related diseases such as obesity and diabetes are traced, at least in part, to our mass production of food. The warnings are clear: because we farm and eat in a way that undermines health and abuses natural resources (to say nothing of the economic and social implications), the conventional food system can't be sustained. Fixtures of agribusiness such as massive grain monocultures and bloated animal feedlots are no more the future of farming than eighteenth-century factories billowing black smoke are the future of manufacturing.

So what is?

More and more studies are showing that diverse, holistic agriculture – with integrated crop and livestock production and proper soil management – is the answer. Not only is this kind of agriculture essential from an ecological point of view, but it also often outperforms the productivity of chemical monocultures in the long term.

But we can't have a discussion about the future of food without talking about how we eat. Even the most forward-thinking farming can't be sustained if our diets don't support it – if we continue along current trends: eating more meat, and more of the center cuts; using our grains for fuel or feed, rather than food.

For the future, our charge as eaters and as cooks is to reconceive our diets to reflect the needs of our landscape – to reimagine the way we eat from the ground up. What kind of menu will move us closer to achieving the Global Goals in 2030? Can we envision a way of eating that not only sustains the world, but also acts as an engine for improvement? There isn't one answer, of course, because it depends on where you live and what time of year it is. However, there are certain shared principals – ingredients put together to become a diet – that will shape this new era of ecological eating.

The menu I describe below is specific to my home (the Northeastern United States), but its core tenets can be applied anywhere.

A MENU FOR 2030

First course: "Landfill Salad"

Our meal of the future will start in the landfill. After all, what better way to begin than with what otherwise would be left behind: the ingredients that have been missing from our menus.

More than a third of all food produced worldwide goes to waste. Approximately 28% of the world's farmland produces food that is never consumed – a staggering loss not only of nutritional potential, but also of natural resources. (It's also a significant contributor to climate change; if food waste were a nation, it would be the third largest emitter of greenhouse gas emissions.)

There are countless factors that contribute to food waste, from field to marketplace. But some of the most glaring examples take place on – or, more to the point, off – our plates. Each year, consumers in high-income countries discard approximately 222 million tons of food. That's just shy of the total net food production of all of sub-Saharan Africa: 230 million tons. The average American family throws out about 25% of the food it buys.

These are incriminating statistics, but also empowering ones. What's clear is that food waste is one arena where consumers have enormous potential to make a change. A "Landfill Salad" is one way to do so. No, this salad won't require foraging in any dumpsters. But it is made up of intercepted ingredients that often end up in our trash cans or compost bins: vegetable scraps such as romaine hearts, carrot ribbons, broccoli cores and radish tops.

Making a dish out of the discarded may not sound very appetizing; but, in fact, with a little attention, these offcuts can be elevated to delicious heights: roasted in olive oil, romaine hearts take on the smoky crunch of Brussels sprouts; radish tops make a peppery pesto vinaigrette.

In essence, this salad honors what most food cultures have done for thousands of years: utilizing creativity and culinary technique to make something delicious out of the ignored or un-coveted. In the future, that approach will become commonplace not just by necessity, but because people will see opportunity in the satisfaction of good cooking. Perhaps "Landfill Salad" is the wrong name. If we do our jobs right, in fifteen years this dish will need a new title because these items will just be an expected part of our everyday eating. The by-products of our food system will be celebrated as flavorful ingredients in their own right.

Second course: "Shellfish and What They Eat"

It's fair to question whether, fifteen years from now, there will be any fish left for our menus. Reports on the state of our oceans show the devastating effect of our appetites. Today, 80% of the world's fish stocks are reported as fully exploited or over-exploited.

Simply put, we take too many fish from the sea. And we take the wrong fish. We demand those large fish at the highest trophic levels. It's little wonder that many of these species, like cod and tuna, have declined by 90% in just the past few decades.

Ensuring the health of these species, and the ocean itself, is going to require more imagination in our sourcing and our cooking. Rather than cherry-picking from the top of the food web, why not start at the bottom, with the wealth of aquatic plants on which all other marine life depends?

Take seaweed, for instance, which in this dish will be infused into an aromatic broth. Recently hailed as the next superfood, seaweed is rich in essential minerals and vitamins. It is also rich with culinary potential; the dozens of known edible varieties easily eclipse the diversity of an all-you-can eat buffet. And we can feel good about indulging. After all, seaweed thrives under sustainable aquaculture conditions, growing quickly without chemical inputs. In fact, it can actually absorb potentially harmful excess nutrients such as carbon, nitrogen and phosphorous, all while increasing oxygen levels – a natural water purification system.

We'll garnish the broth, not with a seven-ounce fillet, but with a variety of filter-feeding shellfish such as oysters and mussels. The result? A footprint-negative plate of food, and a new approach to seafood that will serve to restore our oceans.

Third course: Parsnip Steak, Grass-fed Beef
We don't end most meals these days with a vegetable course, but a generation from now we probably will, or we'll come close. As with everything on this menu of the future, the reason to turn away from a meat-centric main course will be based on the demands of ecology. If our menus are going to work in partnership with what the land can provide, vegetables and grains will inevitably take center stage.

Whether we're talking about a 16-ounce ribeye, a pork chop, or a chicken breast, that choice cut of meat is likely mired in a system that's cruel to animals, is destructive to the environment, and diverts precious resources away from feeding people directly. About 36% of the world's crops go to feeding livestock. In other words, the protein-centric plate of food – a paradigm that America is quickly exporting to the rest of the world – is unsustainable in every sense of the word. And fifteen years from now, it will be a thing of the past.

In place of a hulking center-cut of meat, you'll find a winter parsnip, sweetened from the frost. These days, the humble parsnip is often pushed to the margins of our plates; but, a few decades from now, we'll be showing off the bravura roots by roasting them like steaks.

Meat won't be missing entirely. "Mother Earth never attempts to farm without livestock." That's according to Sir Albert Howard, the father of organic agriculture, and so our plates should include a little livestock, too. But when it does appear, it will do so modestly; it will take up less space on the plate, and, more often than not, it will be a piece of the animal – like neck or shank – that Americans so willingly discard.

So a bit of braised beef shank will act as a kind of garnish for the parsnip, alongside a richly flavored Bordelaise sauce made with the bones. It's a perfect way to create a deeply flavored, resonant dish out of these disparate and lowly cuts, and to turn the iconic steak dinner on its head.

Fourth course: Roasted 898 Squash

The most innovative thing on this menu of the future happens to fit in your hand. It's a small winter squash by the name of 898, created by a cucurbits breeder at Cornell University named Michael Mazourek.

I first met Professor Mazourek several years ago, when he came for dinner at my restaurant. After the meal, he came into the kitchen. I held up a butternut squash (the best-selling workaday winter squash) and, half-jokingly, asked him if

A MENU FOR 2030

FIRST COURSE:
"LANDFILL SALAD"
Vegetable scraps with radish top vinaigrette
*Impact: Combatting food waste by making something
delicious out of the otherwise discarded.*

SECOND COURSE:
"SHELLFISH AND WHAT THEY EAT"
Seaweed broth with filter-feeding shellfish
*Impact: Protecting declining fish species and restoring
oceans by eating from the bottom of the food web.*

THIRD COURSE:
"PARSNIP STEAK, GRASS-FED BEEF"
Roasted parsnip steak, braised beef shank and
Bordelaise sauce
*Impact: Listening to the demands of ecology,
promoting animal welfare and protecting the
environment by moving away from meat-centric
dishes.*

FOURTH COURSE:
"ROASTED 898 SQUASH"
Winter squash created by vegetable breeder
Michael Mazourek
*Impact: Encouraging a new generation of plant
breeders, creating varieties not only based on yield, but
also selected for flavor, nutrition and locality.*

---

he could create a new variety with a more intense squash flavor. He explained that squash breeders are not unlike most modern breeders – they look for the largest market, which means breeding for yield and uniformity, and, in turn, for monocultures and mass distribution.

"It's a funny thing, or maybe a tragic/funny thing," he said, "but in all my years breeding new varieties – after maybe tens of thousands of trials – no one has ever asked me to breed for flavor. Not one person."

Breeders are architects, and seeds are the blueprints for the farming system. Even before farmers actually farm, the seed sets the foundation. If yield and uniformity are the determining factors, then the system, from the field to distributor to marketplace, pretty much falls into place. We say, "It begins with the seed," and really it does, but it also begins with the idea for the seed.

Which is why chefs, farmers, nutritionists, and eaters need to be more involved in their conception. Together we can help encourage a new generation of plant breeders, creating varieties not only based on yield but also selected for flavor, nutrition and locality. And we can breed for the right kind of farming, too. After all, the best plant breeders understand that the system the plant is grown in is just as important as its genetics. If the soil isn't well managed, even the best genetics won't be expressed.

The result may look something like the 898 squash. Still in the selection process, it's been bred for a variety of traits: strong yield and disease resistance, a built-in ripeness indicator (so the farmer knows exactly when to pick it from the vine), and about twice the beta-carotene and other carotenoids as in the average butternut.

Even better? It's naturally sweet (the Brix is a candy-like 15+), making it a delicious and nutritious addition to any dessert cart.

What does the menu of the future look like?

It turns out, it looks a lot like what traditional food cultures around the world figured out thousands of years ago. They did not choose their dietary preferences by sticking a wet finger up to the prevailing wind. Instead, they developed cuisines that adhered to what the landscape could provide. They celebrated diversity, combining tastes not based on convention, but because they fitted together to support the environment that produced them. And they were constantly evolving to reflect the best of what nature could offer.

If we make that the future of food, it's going to be delicious.

Entrepreneurship as an Accelerator

By **Ashish J. Thakkar** *&* **James I. Mwangi**

Ashish Thakkar founded his first business in 1996 at the age of 15 with a US$ 5,000 loan. Since then, he has grown Mara Group from a small IT business in Uganda to a global multi-sector investment group that employs over 11,000 people in 22 African countries, spanning multiple sectors. Born in the UK, Ashish and his family moved back to Africa after surviving the historic Rwandan genocide. Ashish is passionate about mentoring and inspiring young and women entrepreneurs, which led him to create Mara Foundation in 2009.

James Mwangi is Executive Director of the Dalberg Group, a collection of impact-driven businesses that seek to champion inclusive and sustainable growth around the world. A native Kenyan, James founded Dalberg's presence in Africa, beginning with the Johannesburg office in 2007, and now including presences in six offices across the continent, and he also served as Dalberg's Global Managing Partner from 2010 to 2014.

Ashish and James currently serve together on the United Nations Foundation's Global Entrepreneurs Council.

Vibrant entrepreneurship will accelerate progress across the Global Goals. To do so, we must actively support entrepreneurship ecosystems and feed them with early-stage capital, talent and mentorship.

One of the great challenges for today's leaders is creating meaningful employment for our young people. The International Labour Office (ILO) reports global unemployment at over 200 million and notes that the majority of those unemployed are youth (ages 15-24)[1]. The World Economic Forum estimates that over 340 million youth are not working nor in school and that another 536 million young people are working in jobs that don't fully utilize their education and experience[2].

The only way that we're going to create hundreds of thousands of jobs is by placing big bets on small businesses. Small and medium-sized enterprises (SMEs)[3] represent 78% of the jobs in low-income countries[4] and more than 90% of all new jobs created each year[5] – these businesses are the true global engines of employment. Increasing rates of entrepreneurship and accelerating the rate at which ventures grow is the only realistic path to creating enough jobs for the next generation.

Vibrant entrepreneurial ecosystems not only create jobs, they are also fundamental to achieving many of our Global Goals. Entrepreneurship and the job creation that accompanies it are directly linked to the goal of achieving Decent Work and Economic Growth. It also supports progress on the elimination of poverty and hunger and improved health, well-being, and quality education. The same approach helps to address industry, innovation, and infrastructure; and develop new technologies, efficiencies, and ways of communicating to promote affordable and clean energy, and sustainable cities and communities. One example is the Kenyan start-up M-KOPA, which has developed a cost-effective solar home system that by the end of 2015 had brought clean energy to 250,000 homes, via a technology-enabled business model that is both profitable and scalable.

In order to create vibrant entrepreneurial ecosystems, increase job growth, and achieve the Global Goals, a collaborative approach between the public and private sectors is necessary. At the United Nations Foundation's Global Entrepreneurs Council, a body that we are both proud to represent, we focus on how businesses can demonstrate their role in sustainable development. We believe that they can be a powerful force for social good and that entrepreneurship ecosystems offer a chance to maximize private sector value. But in order to ensure this symbiosis, governments need to adopt appropriate policies including tax incentives, labor laws, IP/trademark laws to protect the ideas of entrepreneurs, and formalization of informal enterprises.

In our experience, creating a policy environment conducive to entrepreneurship is necessary, but not sufficient. We must work to ensure that entrepreneurs have access to early-stage capital, mentorship, and skilled talent. Where these ingredients come together effectively, entrepreneurs can be a powerful lever to help societies pursue the Global Goals and create broad-based prosperity.

Early-stage capital is needed for entrepreneurial organizations to establish themselves but is often not available in frontier and emerging markets. That limits entrepreneurship for those who do not have family money to invest. The last few years have seen a large increase in foreign capital in emerging markets. However, these investments are typically for deals in excess of several hundred thousand dollars, while early-stage entrepreneurs seek as little as US$ 5,000. As global conditions have shifted, 2016 has brought much greater skepticism and hesitation about investing in less proven markets. It is important not only to maintain the supply of capital but also tailor it better to smaller and earlier-stage opportunities with some of the best prospects for impact and return.

Effective and relevant mentorship is often crucial to helping entrepreneurs access the advice and support they need to overcome challenges and pursue their vision. When Ashish started his business at age 15, he was able to draw on encouragement and advice from a family with a long track record. Many budding entrepreneurs lack role models in their families and immediate social networks and falter in the absence of positive reinforcement and guidance. Creating effective and accessible mentorship networks around the world could unleash the potential of many who give up.

Appropriately prepared talent is crucial for growing ventures in the challenging environments of many emerging markets. Unfortunately, many of the best-trained and qualified people are directed toward the relative security and status of steady jobs in government and large corporations. At Mara Group, we face challenges when trying to attract talent, especially in our technology startups. For Dalberg, talent is both the biggest binding constraint to our growth and one of the most serious challenges facing our clients. As investors, we understand the risks in placing capital in young companies when few highly skilled people are seeking to become entrepreneurs and even fewer are lining up to become CFOs or marketing executives in early-stage ventures. Interestingly, the dynamic in wealthier countries is increasingly the reverse: the best of the best seek their fortunes in early-stage start-ups where they can find financial rewards while making the difference between success and failure. Addressing this gap will require not only creating channels for new enterprises to access talent but also increasing the appreciation of entrepreneurship in the countries and communities that need it most.

Particular attention must be paid to female entrepreneurs, who face an even steeper challenge in many economies. Seventy percent of women-owned SMEs in developing countries are unserved or under-served by financial institutions[6]. According to predictions by Goldman Sachs, increasing women's access to capital can have a tangible impact on per capita income: if the gender credit gap is closed by 2020, per capita incomes could be on average 12% higher than currently expected across emerging markets by 2030[7]. Nevertheless, Dalberg teams are consistently told by local institutions that "there are no women-led businesses" or that "women-led businesses are not investable.[8]" There is no reason to believe that women entrepreneurs are worse investments than their male counterparts. Common sense suggests that there are more good investments to be found among the underserved pool of female entrepreneurs than their more privileged male counterparts.

Entrepreneurial ecosystems are also missing real opportunities to capitalize on the wealth of eager talent in refugee and migrant populations. As enterprises struggle to attract the talent necessary to scale their businesses and create badly needed jobs, many economies are turning away skilled workers. According to UNHCR, 60 million people were displaced – primarily due to conflict or economic collapse – at the end of 2014, a 14% increase from the previous year and a trend that is expected to continue. The number of refugees today is greater than it has ever been and the percentage of the world's population displaced is higher than at any time since the end of the Second World War. Tellingly, many of today's most successful companies trace their roots to refugees, including Intel (co-founder Andy Grove fled Hungary to the US) and Marks and Spencer (co-founder Michael Marks fled Russia to the UK). Sadly, the international community has been slow to accept the gift of an influx of talent. Syrian refugees, for example, have struggled to find asylum and have only been able to do so under a humanitarian banner, even though over half of Syrian refugees are skilled or semi-skilled workers[9].

We believe there are four key actions that can be taken now to strengthen entrepreneurship ecosystems and accelerate our progress towards the Global Goals:

- Dramatically increase the availability of early-stage capital in emerging and frontier markets. Innovations will be required in order to deploy small amounts of capital at scale; these innovations should be a priority for governments, investors and development partners. Opportunities exist to increase the availability of debt by developing new financial infrastructure (such as credit rating agencies) that reduces the cost of lending, or by introducing new models of deploying capital through business accelerators to leverage knowledge of their clients in reducing credit risks. It should also be possible to increase equity capital by bringing diaspora investment dollars home, and to innovate around crowdfunding platforms. Most importantly, broadening the net of financial inclusion in developing countries could add hundreds of billions of dollars in savings, denominated in local currencies, to the pool of capital available for banks to lend to small enterprises. Public policy decisions could drive considerable capital into early-stage businesses.

For example, state-run pension funds could be mandated to invest a certain portion of their assets in early-stage companies. Programs that incentivize successful local entrepreneurs to engage in more angel investment – perhaps by fostering technical capacity, providing leverage for personal funding, or sharing risk – would go a long way toward intermediating smaller investments. We should be innovating new ways to fund start-up enterprises, and advocating for appropriate policies to incentivize this work.

- Start mentoring our young entrepreneurs and treating them as the leaders they are. Over the last twenty years, organizations such as Endeavor, Ashoka, Echoing Green, PopTech and the Unreasonable Institute have selected entrepreneurs for special programs and linked them to mentors. While the number of entrepreneurs reached remains far fewer than are needed, their success in empowering a new set of leaders is beginning to pay dividends. Mara Foundation has launched Mara Mentor, which seeks to scale mentorship with an online platform and mobile application allowing ambitious entrepreneurs to connect with peers and business leaders. It empowers them to build their businesses and inspires them by facilitating a collaborative approach to business start-up and growth, while dramatically expanding the pool of mentors available to start-up companies. We should encourage experienced professionals to commit to mentorship and continue to innovate platforms to enable them to do so.

- Develop latent talent in emerging markets to feed the under-served global demand for effective managers and technical

The employment challenge

Inadequately educated workforce and lack of access to appropriate finance are major constraints to small businesses globally

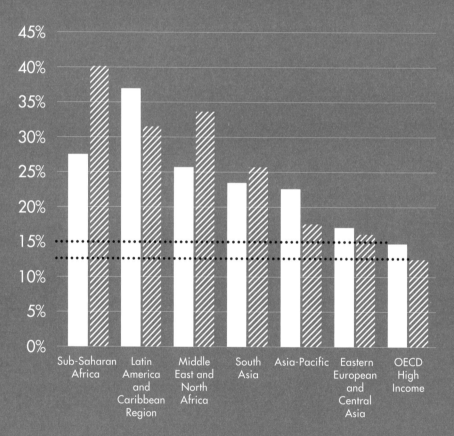

% of SMEs identifying an inadequately educated workforce as a major constraint

% of SMEs identifying access to finance as a major constraint

Source: World Bank Enterprise Survey, calculated using most recent survey available for all countries where surveys are available, only small and medium size firms included.

73.4 million youth worldwide are unemployed*

17.9%

11.2%

13.9%

30.7%   29%   10%

11.6%

13.6%

● Regional youth unemployment rates**

Source: ILO, Global Employment Trends for Youth, 2015
Note: * 2015 (projection) ** 2016 (projection). Youth unemployment rate in the EU and other developed economies is 15.7%

talent. We believe that the skills and aptitudes needed to grow a vibrant enterprise are spread relatively evenly across the world. Businesses should be working to identify and invest in this talent within the large pool of unemployed youth. Instead, they irrationally compete with one another for talent from the same universities, neighborhoods and populations that they always have. Andela is a technology company that has sought to profit from this inefficiency. The company attracts high-potential technical talent in Nigeria and Kenya, puts them through a rigorous screening process (accepting only 1% of applicants), provides world class training and then places graduates in technology companies for a fee. In South Africa, Harambee Youth Employment Accelerator is an NGO founded by a consortium of corporations to identify and train high-potential first-time workers for entry-level skills. They are now seeking to send graduates into SMEs by standardizing a set of common roles (e.g., sales clerk or bookkeeper), assessing and then offering training and jobs. We should encourage businesses to search for aptitude in new places and actively support the creation of intermediaries to facilitate this process.

- Increase investment in overlooked entrepreneurs, most importantly women and refugees. In 2014, Goldman Sachs and the International Finance Corporation partnered to create a US$ 600 million fund to work with banks around the world to ensure that appropriate financing products are accessible to female entrepreneurs. At Mara Foundation, we are partnering with UN Women and combining our respective expertise to ensure that women entrepreneurs can overcome the challenges they face. Chobani Yogurt started by Hamdi Ulukaya, a Kurdish migrant from Turkey, and is now one of the largest food service businesses in the United States. In 2008, he began staffing his Upstate New York plants with refugees, and he now employs over 300. He finds their work ethic and diverse backgrounds make them ideal employees. We should work to ensure that all would-be entrepreneurs have access to the support, financing and mentorship they need to be successful. We should also support our entrepreneurs in tapping into overlooked pools of talent.

We believe that entrepreneurial ecosystems behave as virtuous cycles and that accelerating today's entrepreneurs will pay dividends in years to come. Today's entrepreneurs are tomorrow's mentors and angel investors. As an entrepreneurial ecosystem reaches scale, financial, legal and educational structures can better support it. If we take the four steps identified in this chapter, we will be creating an endowment of entrepreneurial talent that will help accelerate progress across the majority of the Global Goals for years to come. This is not only a moral imperative for our generation, but also an attractive business opportunity.

---

1. International Labour Office (ILO). World Employment Social Outlook, 2015
2. World Economic Forum. Youth Unemployment Visualization, 2013
3. Definitions of SME vary; however, the World Bank defines SMEs as businesses that have fewer than 300 employees, earn less than US$ 15 million in annual revenue, and have less than US$ 15 million in assets
4. ILO and GIZ. Is Small Still Beautiful?, 2013
5. Ayyagari, Meghana, Asli Demirguc-Kunt, and Vojislav Maksimovic. Small vs. Young Firms across the World Contribution to Employment, Job Creation, and Growth. World Bank, 2011
6. International Finance Corporation (IFC). Strengthening Access to Finance for Women-Owned SMEs in Developing Countries. October, 2011
7. Goldman Sachs. Giving Credit Where It Is Due. March, 2014
8. Kakar, Yana Watson (Dalberg). "Inclusion Versus Innovation," Huffington Post, August 9, 2013
9. Based on a 2013 ILO survey of Syrian refugees in Jordan

Establishing a GPS to Chart Progress Towards the Global Goals – and Keep Them on Track

By **Angel Gurría**

Angel Gurría has been the Secretary-General of the OECD since June 2006. As OECD Secretary-General, he has reinforced the OECD's role as a 'hub' for global dialogue and debate on economic policy issues while pursuing internal modernization and reform. Mr. Gurría is a Mexican national and came to the OECD following a distinguished career in public service in his country, including positions as Minister of Foreign Affairs and Minister of Finance and Public Credit in the 1990s. Mr. Gurría holds a B.A. degree in Economics from UNAM (Mexico) and a M.A. degree in Economics from Leeds University (United Kingdom). He is married and has three children.

One of the key requirements for implementing the Global Goals is in development finance, in particular measuring, monitoring, and mobilizing resources. The financing framework underpinning the ambitious agenda requires a broad suite of financial resources, including aid, domestic resources, foreign and domestic investments, blended finance, remittances, and philanthropy. By deploying a multi-disciplinary approach, leveraging policy frameworks, comparative assessments and measurement tools, it will be possible to establish a Global Positioning System (GPS) for finance flows that not only captures the immediate status quo of development resources, but also highlights pathways and direction for future action.

The global community has an unprecedented opportunity over the next 15 years to create a more inclusive and sustainable future for all. Now that world leaders have collectively agreed upon what the Global Goals aim to achieve, the international debate on how to achieve and finance the agenda must deliver a robust implementation strategy. Agreements may make the headlines, but the implementation is what will change lives. We need to help countries reach the point of successful implementation if we are going to deliver on the promises of 2015.

Successful implementation will depend on sound public policies in many areas. This includes policies to help mobilize all available assets – finance, tools, knowledge, and partnerships. To support our public policy efforts, there is a need to establish a GPS for the Global Goals. A GPS knows where you are, and if you tell it where you want to go, it tells you the best route. If you get lost, it gets you back on track. A GPS for the Global Goals will do exactly this by leveraging data, tools and indicators that can help countries determine where they currently stand, and which pathways are available to fulfil their commitment. At the OECD, this is a core aspiration. This is a big bet for the implementation of the Global Goals.

Aid alone is not enough to deliver on the Global Goals

When it comes to financing the Goals, aid is and will remain a crucial resource to finance sustainable development, particularly in countries most in need. However, aid alone – which reached an all-time high of US$ 137.2 billion from the Development Assistance Committee (DAC) member countries in 2014 – is insufficient to fulfil the financing needs of the Global Goals, which total trillions of dollars annually[1]. The financing framework underpinning the ambitious Global Goals agenda requires a broad suite of financial resources for developing countries, including not just aid but also domestic resources, foreign and domestic investments, blended finance, remittances, and philanthropy.

Domestic resource mobilization, including taxation, is a centerpiece of the financing for development agenda. Domestic resources provide by far the largest share of finance for development and will increasingly be the pillar of sustainable growth and poverty eradication.

Remittances are vital as well. They constitute the second

largest source of international financial flows to developing countries after foreign direct investment and are more stable than other flows over economic cycles. Measures to enhance the productive use of remittances include lowering transfer costs, ensuring that adequate and affordable financial services are available to migrants and their families, and increasing financial inclusion and literacy.

Finally, not to be overlooked are philanthropic flows, which can be instrumental in leveraging other sources of funding, providing early stage capital to social entrepreneurs and supporting impact investment. Philanthropic foundations range from individual or family-based foundations, of which there are over 36,000 in the United States alone, to more established and corporate foundations, as well as a bold and new set of philanthropists from the global south[2]. These resources need to be mobilized further in support of the new development agenda.

The OECD can be a GPS for all these sources of financing for development

The OECD measures progress in all of these areas, guiding and assessing countries as they strive to meet the Global Goals. Supporting a development landscape, which goes beyond aid, we are collaborating with partners to develop a new measurement framework, known as Total Official Support for Sustainable Development (TOSSD). The framework helps track sources of development finance, most notably public resources, and broader private finance, from domestic and international sources. A more comprehensive measurement framework will contribute to international standards and norms and enrich understanding of the totality of sustainable development finance flows available for implementation of the Global Goals.

However, public resources, including aid, are not enough. There is also a huge, and largely untapped, potential for public, philanthropic and private actors to work together towards win-win solutions, which provide a good return on investment and which transform economies, societies and lives towards a better future. Here, the OECD and a number of other players are increasingly engaging with philanthropic capital as a source of development finance.

Although guaranteeing investments and supplementing private investment with grant financing can incentivize investment and reduce perceived risks, effective financing strategies to fund the Global Goals in individual countries will still require transparency and enhanced public-private dialogue in combining the diverse resource flows in the mix.

Here, the GPS analogy is fitting. By using the TOSSD framework and continuously expanding and improving the data collection and analyses behind it, national governments, NGOs, philanthropic organizations and international institutions will be able to drive targeted and impactful decision-making around the Global Goals.

Concretely, I see four core steps towards a fully operational GPS for development finance, capable of providing not only a snapshot of a country's current location but also providing information about the route ahead:

Resource flows from OECD-DAC members to developing countries in 2014

$398 bn

PRIVATE FLOWS AT MARKET TERMS

Private flows at market terms, comprising foreign direct investment and other securities from OECD-DAC members

$137 bn

OFFICIAL DEVELOPMENT ASSISTANCE

Official development assistance, comprising flows from OECD-DAC members

$123 bn

PERSONAL REMITTANCES

The estimated share of remittance flows from OECD-DAC members using the World Bank Bilateral Remittance Matrix

$32 bn

**PRIVATE
GRANTS**

Private grants,
comprising grants from
private philanthropic
foundations and NGOs

$6 bn

**OFFICIALLY
SUPPORTED
EXPORT CREDITS**

Officially supported
export credits,
comprising direct
export credits and
export credit
guarantees/insurance

$3 bn

**NON-
CONCESSIONAL
OFFICIAL
DEVELOPMENT
FINANCE**

Non-concessional
official development
finance, comprising
flows from
OECD-DAC members

Source: OECD-DAC Statistics

- Develop new measurement frameworks to measure, monitor and mobilize financing for development taking the new Global Goal indicators into account.
- Support one integrated global platform, drawing on all relevant stakeholders for reporting, reviewing and knowledge sharing on the multiple sources of sustainable development finance.
- Mobilize philanthropic flows by incentivizing various development actors and breaking down silos between public and private stakeholders.
- Identify relevant and coherent development financing policies and incentives to mobilize resources – public, private, domestic, and foreign – in mutually reinforcing ways.

If these steps are taken by the OECD, in partnership with our member countries and development partners, the global community will be in a better position to deliver on the Global Goals.

Looking to the future, we will play a critical role in supporting global platforms. For instance, as a member of the Addis Inter-Agency Task Force (IATF), the OECD will contribute to monitoring and reviewing progress to deliver the means of implementation agreed upon in Addis Ababa in July 2015. Similarly, we are working on a new flagship report – *The Global Outlook on Development Finance* – which will provide a methodology for assessing and integrating the range of financing resources to address the social, economic, and environmental dimensions of sustainable development in an integrated manner. This will be a next step to develop the TOSSD framework further.

The mobilization of sufficient resources remains one of the global community's top challenges as we collectively embark upon the implementation journey of the Global Goals. The OECD's big bet is to rise to the challenge and provide the GPS that our member countries and development partners need to help turn 2015's promises into a better, greener, fairer future for all.

---

1. Final Official Development Assistance Figures in 2014, http://www.oecd.org
2. Philanthropy and Youth Empowerment: Foundations' Innovative Approaches to Support Youth, OECD 2014, p.16

Knowledge for Knowledge's Sake Is the Most Valuable Commodity We Possess

By **Fabiola Gianotti**

Fabiola Gianotti joined CERN (European Organization for Nuclear Research) in 1994 and became the first female Director-General of CERN in 2016. She holds an honorary Professorship at Edinburgh University and is a corresponding member of the Italian Academy of Sciences and foreign associate member of the US Academy of Sciences and the French Academy of Sciences. From 2009 to 2013, she was project leader ("spokesperson") for the ATLAS experiment, and on July 4, 2012, she presented the collaboration's results in a seminar at CERN where the discovery of the Higgs boson was announced. In 2011, Gianotti was included among *The Guardian* newspaper's 100 most inspirational women. She ranked 5th in *Time* magazine's Personality of the Year in 2012 and appeared among *Forbes* magazine's 100 most influential women in 2013.

Basic research is often considered to be a luxury, yet it is the most valuable asset we have, underpinning innovation from the harnessing of fire to the technologies we will need to deliver a sustainable future. Not all efforts towards the fulfilment of the new Global Goals need to be short-term, practical and focused. Basic science, and the opportunity to invent and innovate from the very bottom, often provide the knowledge needed to drive more significant and structural changes for the greater good.

As far back as 1939, Abraham Flexner penned a stirring paean to basic research in *Harper's* magazine under the title: 'The Usefulness of Useless Knowledge'. Nine years earlier, Flexner had been among the founders of the Institute for Advanced Studies (IAS) in Princeton, New Jersey, a temple to 'useless' knowledge, and his article recounts a conversation he had with a certain Mr. George Eastman. In short, Flexner had asked Eastman whom he considered to be the most useful worker in the world, to which Eastman replied instantaneously: "Marconi." There the disagreement began. Flexner, perhaps being intentionally provocative, pointed out that Marconi's contribution to the radio and wireless had been practically negligible. He went on to point out the 1865 work of James Clerk Maxwell on the theoretical underpinnings of electricity and magnetism, and the subsequent experimental work of Heinrich Hertz on the detection of electromagnetic waves. Maxwell and Hertz, he argued, had no concern about the practical utility of their work; they cared only about the adding to the shared pool of knowledge about the workings of the natural world. The knowledge they sought, in other words, was never intended to be useful. Without it, however, there could have been no Marconi, no wireless, no radio, no television and no mobile phones.

The history of innovation is full of such examples. Indeed, it is practically impossible to find a piece of technology that cannot be traced back to the work of scientists motivated purely by a desire to understand the world we inhabit. But basic research goes further. There is something primordial about it. Every child is a natural scientist, imbued with curiosity, vivid imagination and a desire to learn. It is what sets us apart from any other species, and it is what has provided the wellspring of innovation since early humans harnessed fire and invented wheels. Children are always asking questions. Why is the sky blue? What are we made of? What are those specks of twinkling light in the night sky? It's by investigating questions like these that science has advanced, and that we can inspire the young to grow up into future scientists or scientifically aware citizens.

To demonstrate this, let me highlight one particular example that I know very well: The Brout-Englert-Higgs mechanism. The research that led to its elucidation in 2012 with the discovery of the Higgs boson at CERN was inspired by the question: "Why do some forces of nature, like Maxwell's electromagnetism, have an infinite range, while others act only over short distances, like those that work on the scale of the atomic nucleus?" You will not find a more esoteric question, yet when we announced the discovery of the Higgs boson on July 4, 2012, it was covered by media, including social media, around the world with great excitement. In the case of the Brout-Englert-Higgs mechanism, the time between asking the question and finding the answer was 50 years and encompassed many cycles of knowledge transfer from basic to applied research and back again.

Indeed, the ambitious goals of fundamental research require the development, construction, and operation of high-tech, complex instruments that challenge industry to push the limits of technology. Such innovations in the name of fundamental science frequently make their way to society. One strong example of this is a thread stretching back to the 1970s, linking CERN with the medical imaging industry. Back then, CERN had a collaboration with its local hospital to apply CERN photon and electron detection technology to the task of developing one of the very first PET scanners. The latest chapter in this story comes with the development of electronics that allow photon and electron detectors to be read out in a strong magnetic field. This not only provides the powerful capacity for experiments at CERN but has also enabled the medical imaging industry to develop combined PET/MRI scanners, thereby improving medical diagnosis techniques. This is fundamental research having a profound and positive impact on people's lives around the world.

Two things become very obvious when you observe physicists at work. Firstly, the word impossible is not in their vocabulary. In this case, when they found that the electronics that worked in a magnetic field didn't exist, there was no question of giving up. The obvious thing to do was develop these electronics. And the second thing you notice is that they don't care about things like gender, ethnicity and race: what matters is simply how good you are at what you do. Nothing comes closer to a true meritocracy than a particle physics experiment, and the results are extraordinary. It's the strength of these very diverse collaborations that delivers developments such as magnetic field-tolerant electronics.

Nurturing such curious minds is among CERN's core missions. We take education and training very seriously, and over the years have developed programs that reach everyone from primary school children to professional physicists, accelerator scientists, and computer scientists. We also keep tabs on the whereabouts of young people passing through CERN, and it is very enriching to follow their progress. About a thousand people a year receive higher degrees from universities around the world for work carried out at CERN. Just over a third of them remain in public sector research, while the rest take their experience into other walks of life. Basic science therefore not only inspires young people to study science, it also provides a steady stream of qualified people for business and industry, where their high-tech, international experience allows them to make a positive impact around the world.

Turning to the UN's admirably ambitious Global Goals, the focus on science and technology in Agenda 2030 is positive and encouraging. It testifies to a deeper understanding of the importance of science in driving progress that benefits all people and helps to overcome today's most pressing development challenges. But the potential of Agenda 2030 can only be fulfilled if backed by sustained commitment and funding by governments. I contend that if we are to tackle issues from eliminating poverty and hunger to providing clean and affordable energy, we need science, and we need scientifically-aware citizens. That's why the input from the scientific community, including CERN, to framing Agenda 2030 urged there to be a minimum percentage of GDP devoted by every nation to science and STEM education (Science, Technology, Engineering and Math education), with the

Quantum mechanics and Einstein's relativity: who needs them?

Quantum mechanics and Einstein's relativity are widely perceived to be among the most esoteric, abstruse and impractical areas of science, yet most of us rely on them every day. Around 100 years ago, Einstein and other great minds developed them into the pillars of 20th century physics. The general theory of relativity describes gravity, and received a ringing endorsement earlier this year with the discovery of gravitational waves, predicted by Einstein in 1915. As such, it can be thought of as the theory that explains the large-scale behavior of the universe we inhabit. Quantum mechanics, on the other hand, is the theory of the very small. It describes the behavior of the fundamental particles that we, and everything visible in the universe, are made of. Both are extremely well established and painstakingly experimentally verified theories.

The people who developed these ideas were motivated only by the desire to know: a desire that is common to all humanity, and that distinguishes us from any other living thing on the planet. We're a curious and imaginative species and collectively attach great value to know-ledge in all its forms.

This curiosity has stood us in good stead. It has underpinned everything from the harnessing of fire to the development of agriculture and indeed anything that bears the label technology today. In the case of quantum mechanics, the entire modern electronics industry depends on it, and in the case of relativity, the GPS positioning system relies upon it to deliver pinpoint geographical accuracy. So the next time you take out your GPS-enabled phone, remember it's a quantum-relativistic machine, and say a word of thanks to the pioneering thinkers whose curiosity and ingenuity made it possible.

public sector committing in particular to basic research and STEM education. We also pointed out that this is particularly important in times of economic downturn when private funding naturally concentrates on short-term payback and governments also focus on domains that offer immediate economic return at the expense of the longer term investment in fundamental science. Governments should always ensure a constant flow of Abraham Flexner's useless knowledge.

Places like CERN are a vitally important ingredient in the innovation chain. We contribute to the kind of knowledge that not only enriches humanity but also provides the wellspring of ideas that become the technologies of the future. We train young people, and we develop technologies ourselves that have immediate applications for the benefit of society: technologies like the World Wide Web and the application of particle accelerators, one of CERN's core areas of expertise, to fields as diverse as food sterilization and cancer therapy.

All this is possible because governments support STEM education and basic research. But we should do more: we should aim to ring-fence a minimum investment in STEM education and basic research in GDP terms for every country in the world. That is the way to long-term development and sustainability.

Flexner's article contains many examples of the usefulness of useless knowledge: knowledge for knowledge's sake. It does not, however, record whether Mr. George Eastman was convinced by his arguments. Whatever the case, history has been kind to Mr. Flexner. The IAS is as strong an ideas factory today as it was in the 1930s, whereas the company Mr. Eastman founded has suffered a rather different fate. Useless knowledge, as Mr. Flexner called it, is at the basis of human development. Humankind's continuing pursuit of it will make the development goals achievable.

A New Era of Collaboration – a Big Bet on Match-Making

By **Mogens Lykketoft**

On June 15 2015, the UN General Assembly elected Mogens Lykketoft to serve as the President of its 70th session, running from September 2015 to September 2016. At the time of his election, Mr. Lykketoft had been the Speaker of the Danish Parliament (since 2011). Mr. Lykketoft is an economist by education and a veteran parliamentarian, serving as leader of the Danish Social Democratic Party from 2002 to 2005. A Cabinet Minister for a total of 11 years, Mr. Lykketoft has served as Minister for Taxation (1980-1981), Minister of Finance (1993-2000), and most recently Minister of Foreign Affairs (2000-2001).

The Sustainable Development Goals framework is itself a big bet – a universal, inclusive and comprehensive approach to development, which not only requires action by everyone but also benefits everyone. In order to implement its sustainable development vision over the next 15 years, a more explicit big bet is proposed: to establish an inclusive platform under the UN to drive alliances for implementation. A Sustainable Development Goals[1] Match Up initiative would match one or more Goals with relevant governmental or non-governmental partners.

For the first time in history, world leaders have agreed on a global framework for sustainable development, with a clear vision to end poverty, empower people and populations, promote a sustainable economy and protect our planet. The framework constitutes a big bet in itself, as it prescribes a path for development entirely different from the one we have followed for the past 15 years. In many ways, the Global Goals are a novelty.

First, the Goals are universal. They cut across geography and apply to every nation, stakeholder and person around the globe. They require action by all, going beyond aid and traditional approaches such as north versus south. They entail a shared responsibility to make the world a better place.

Second, the Goals are inclusive. They are arguably a product of the greatest consultation ever in global politics. Unlike the Millennium Development Goals (MDG) and so many past international agreements, they were drawn up in an inclusive, participatory setting. The normative process took place under the auspices of the UN General Assembly, but was preceded by an innovative process designed to overcome the limitations of the rules of procedure of the General Assembly, which restrict participation to the member states. Through the Open Working Group process, the Global Goals were formulated with the inclusion of an extensive set of stakeholders – parliamentarians, religious leaders and communities, cities and local communities, civil society, youth, trade unions, business, and academia worldwide. Going forward, we need all these core players to keep ambition high, to respond to the reality on the ground, and to remind us to leave no one behind. Now, as we move to execution, we need them to help make our Global Goals a reality. In my view, this is where the UN can play a central role.

Third, the Global Goals are complex and comprehensive. For the first time in history, we now have an agenda anchored in 17 goals, with 169 accompanying indicators, which are interlinked and comprehensive. To create a movement around something complex is never easy and some even argue that the new agenda is too ambitious and that we will not be able to address all goals at the same time. I profoundly disagree. The framework recognizes that complex challenges require comprehensive solutions.

We will not be able to eradicate poverty if we do not create more equality between rich and poor people, alleviate huge economic gaps between developed and emerging countries, and fight discrimination against women, girls and ethnic, social, sexual and religious minorities. Similarly, we will not be able to eradicate poverty if we hesitate to take firm action on the causes of environmental catastrophes and degradation, or neglect the severe consequences of climate change that will drive hundreds of millions of people from their homes and potentially foster new conflicts, further depleting the resources needed for development. We need to respond to the direct links between peace and security, human rights and sustainable development.

In my view, the strength of the Global Goals lies in these original aspects – the universality, the inclusiveness and the complexity. Their success will depend on how exactly we manage and implement them in a process that starts now - and with full force! So how do we do this?

A new era of collaboration

My big bet is to change our overall approach to implementation. We need solutions that are integrated and comprehensive. We need to accept that these changes will require difficult policy choices and decisions on possible trade-offs at all levels. And – most importantly – we need to accept a new era of collaboration.

Sustainable development and persistent global challenges do not respect national borders. Neither can our solutions. The new era of collaboration requires action at the global level, nationally, regionally and locally. This is widely accepted by leaders today.

What is perhaps not so widely accepted is that the existing challenges will not be overcome without a new level of collaboration within and among countries and governments. Governments must show the necessary leadership and take ownership, but alone they cannot bring about the transformation needed. We need the broadest set of stakeholders engaged and working towards the same objective: achievement of the Global Goals.

Addressing hunger, food security, and nutrition, for example, requires the engagement of local actors and individual producers as well as international collaboration in trade, financing, and technological diffusion. It also demands that we address consumption and production patterns; that we engage the private sector; and that local and national governments provide an enabling environment for their activities. Another example is the increasing role of cities and the call for their sustainability. Sustainable cities require the engagement of mayors and local decision-makers in addressing energy, water, infrastructure and food supplies. They need to regulate the use of the underlying natural resources feeding the city and ensuring inclusive approaches to addressing citizens' needs for health care, education and access to public life.

So what does a new era of collaboration look like?

For me, it all comes down to the capabilities of the UN. The UN is a political and moral beacon for its member states, and it should continue to work hand in hand with governments that need multilateral support.

Moving forward, we need to build on and reflect the principles and mechanisms behind the Open Working Group setup. While the normative and legislative fora for member states – the General Assembly and to some degree the Economic Social Council – are not bodies that actually implement, the   UN member states need to create a UN that provides the venue and platform for convening central stakeholders within each Global Goal and each target. In this way, they will create a platform for matching the goals with clear-cut and responsible implementers. The UN needs to be effective, relevant and inspirational. We need to break down the walls that prevent the world's citizens and stakeholders from becoming part of the UN system.

The UN should become the hub or center of a network that brings in all the stakeholders in a variable geometry of alliances configured to each of the Global Goals. Each alliance would constitute a spoke in the wheel that would bring in much larger global forces in civil society, the private sector, academia, parliaments and organizations at a regional or local level. We need to give attention to coherence and the cross-cutting nature of implementation and develop the organizational tools to bring together all the relevant stakeholders. In short, we have to find ways to reduce barriers to increasing and organizing stakeholder engagement.

My unique role as President of the UN General Assembly offers exactly this convening power. My big bet will be to gather everyone to unite around Global Goals implementation and collaboration. We do not need new partnerships or an alternative to the UN. We need the re-invigoration and re-tooling of the UN to enable it to support the new agenda. To this end, I see a platform containing three initiatives, for the UN membership to agree:

First, we need an effective accountability framework. We must develop measures of accountability, vetting and due diligence for all stakeholders. Countries must meet the promises they have made on the Global Goals. Goal 17 explicitly stresses the need for good, timely and reliable data

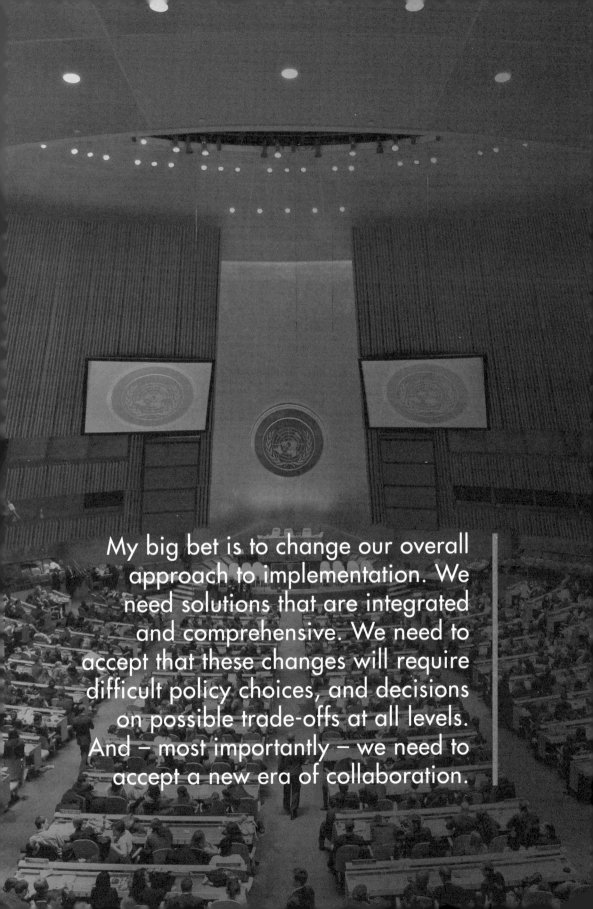

My big bet is to change our overall approach to implementation. We need solutions that are integrated and comprehensive. We need to accept that these changes will require difficult policy choices, and decisions on possible trade-offs at all levels. And – most importantly – we need to accept a new era of collaboration.

that can be disaggregated by income, gender, race, migratory status and so on. Big data, technology, and new visualization tools allow us to track progress in new ways. Transparency International has already shown the way by providing practical tools that weaken opportunities for corruption in the public and private sectors. We need similar approaches.

Second, we have to establish an open platform where individuals and civil society can be engaged. AVAAZ, Kiva, and others have shown the scope for seeking local solutions to global challenges.

Third, we need an ongoing way to create alliances around the Global Goals to develop technologies and solutions. Governments, companies, NGOs and foundations alike should be invited to participate. I propose a Global Goals Match Up initiative for governments with non-governmental partners around each goal. I have already organized such events, and I propose to host a networking session every year – not to track progress on the Global Goals but to support and supplement implementation and collaboration towards our common objective.

Getting people together at yet another UN meeting might not sound like much, but it lies at the heart of the role of the President of the General Assembly. Bringing groups together from different sectors for informal conversations can make things happen, including identifying blockages in technology, infrastructure, financing and partnerships.

Walk the talk

At the UN, I have very quickly realized that we often have way too much talk and too little action and delivery. We need to create the space and inspirational platform to get stakeholders to walk the talk.

Success in the very short term should not be measured in goals and targets met, but new alliances being forged, initiatives launched, action kick-started, and stakeholders included. The outcome of my big bet will hopefully see the emergence of new partnerships on implementation, funding matched with solutions, and gaps in implementation identified and bridged. Implementing the goals will cost trillions of dollars, but convening actors around a single platform and spurring new cooperation does not need to cost much money. What is crucial is the willingness and engagement of partners to come together to deliver concrete action. I believe the will is there. We just need to give them the opportunity to find each other.

In 15 years, I hope we can look back and say the big bet on collaboration got us off to a good start and helped this generation to reach the Global Goals and realize its incredible potential. If it does, new generations enjoy all the possibilities of a life in a peaceful, harmonious and prosperous world. If not, human civilization will be facing existential threats.

---

1. Sustainable Development Goals (SDGs) are equivalent to what is called the Global Goals in this book

How to Score the Global Goals? It's about Justice and Security, Stupid.

By **Jamie Drummond**

Jamie Drummond is a "Factivist" who co-founded ONE, a global pressure group with over 7 million members around the world, which fights against the injustice of extreme poverty. Right now, we're campaigning against corruption and for smart investments in health, nutrition, agriculture, connectivity, and girls' and women's economic empowerment. We're also campaigning for more and better data to inform policy and people. Before, Jamie was the Global Strategist for Drop the Debt (which helped cancel US$ 110 billion of mainly African debt) and co-founder of DATA. org (which helped double smart aid and boost trade deals for Africa).

Jamie Drummond offers an ambitious big bet: build and invest in the mother and daughter of all movements – to help humanity face off an existential threat and seize a historic opportunity. It is an incomplete "open draft" campaign plan to provoke debate and seek input and feedback. Failure to challenge, debate and enact such a campaign plan to achieve the new Global Goals may leave the world a far darker place by 2030.

The Global Goals for Sustainable Development must be radically repositioned, and effective advocacy for the goals must be properly funded, or they will fail. As things stand, there is a risk they will be dismissed as a vague, well-intentioned, lofty UN do-gooders' to-do list, preaching to the converted within the New York/UN development bubble. Instead they must be understood as an essential investment in shared human security, an aggressive and measurable agenda for collective action to counter a profound existential threat faced by our species over the next generation. This piece argues that we can and must build a powerful global movement focused on achieving the goals. It suggests three cross-cutting components of the Global Goals that require deeper focus: extreme poverty; gender justice; and peace, security and combating corruption (Goal 1, Goal 5 and Goal 16). By channeling citizens' anger, or challenging their apathy, and pointing towards positive, practical action, we can recruit a powerful movement for change which will best deliver the goals' key measurable outcomes across health, hunger, malnutrition, education, sustainability, and beyond. If we do not implement such a campaign plan, the goals and the chance for this gneration to change course will be lost.

The existential emergency – human security in the balance

Around the world, billions of citizens are networked and connected as never before, capable of sharing ideas, scaling proven solutions and taking actions together for a better and safer world. But billions more still live in extreme poverty, in regions also stressed by extreme climate and extreme ideologies – sparking ever more tension and conflict in the world's most resource-scarce and climatically and ideologically vulnerable regions, such as Africa's Sahel region. These regions will spread instability just as under-investment in their health systems spreads new viruses from AIDS to Ebola and Zika. Over time, extreme poverty will be most entrenched in Africa, with four-fifths of humans in extreme poverty forecast to be living there by 2030. By 2050, there will be over one billion more citizens of African nations, and 2.5 billion people in Africa in total. By then 37% of the world's youth will be African. Their youthful dynamism could fuel global prosperity, but if blocked by poverty and corrupt governance, their frustration will explode with consequences for everyone. The Sahel is particularly burdened by the "three extremes": extreme poverty, extreme climate, and extreme ideology. From Boko Haram in the West to Al Shabaab in the East, extremists are doing well and will thrive still more if we don't back African plans to end the conditions they feed off. Europe can scarcely cope with the humanitarian crisis posed by Syria today. If the Sahel is destabilized, as its population booms, many more millions of desperate refugees will flood to their neighbors in Africa and the north, risking real de-stabilization of Africa and Europe for a generation. So it is not just morally right but strategically far more sensible to dramatically scale up support for regions like the Sahel now, than suffer the far greater consequences of inaction later.

The choice for each of us is this: do you want to be a passive observer of events and risk such awful global results, or to be an effective global citizen campaigning for change?

At ONE, with our partners, we have some experience of scaled global campaigning for change. We achieve it both on the "inside" through smart policy and political influencing strategies in many countries at once, and on the "outside" through leveraging popular culture and organizing people to speak up at key moments to have the greatest impact on policy and political decisions. This approach has already helped us secure over US\$ 100 billion in debt relief mainly for the poorest African nations, a doubling in smart aid for Africa and laws to boost trade and investment and beat back corruption, altogether helping our partners reduce child mortality dramatically – with over 10,000 fewer children dying per day between 2000 and 2015.

The "Outside" – public campaign and communications strategy

Poverty is Sexist
Women and girls the world over face huge injustices. Today 1,000 teenage girls in Africa will catch HIV largely from predatory older men and hundreds of young would-be mothers will bleed needlessly and painfully to death

in childbirth; this year three million girls will die from preventable, treatable diseases and half a billion women are excluded from opportunity because they cannot read or write, own a phone or open a bank account. Their continued impoverishment hurts them, but it also holds back their families and communities and keeps their countries fragile and in poverty. Addressing these outrageous wrongs will help end extreme poverty in the world's most marginalized regions, with knock-on benefits for security and prosperity the world over.

One response is the Poverty is Sexist campaign, which harnesses these arguments to give the injustice of extreme poverty a newer, more specific identity and energize a generation of "new feminist" activists actions for change. The movement already includes leaders like Melinda Gates, Sheryl Sandberg, Michelle Obama, Angela Merkel, Emma Watson, Chimamanda Ngozie Adichie, Beyonce, Roxane Philson, Lena Dunham, Eloise Todd, Nachilala Nkombo and a teenage girl called Eva Tolage. Eva is 16 years old and lives in remote rural Tanzania. Last year she wrote to ONE's seven million members seeking a partnership to eradicate extreme poverty in all villages like hers. Poverty endures because she is held back: she is hungry at school so cannot study, there is no running water so she must walk 12 km to collect it, there is no electricity and no connectivity and no local bank. The local police are corrupt and resources are increasingly scarce, fueling local ethnic tension. She is determined to change all this. In every village and town, there's a generation of Eva's determined to hold us all accountable and drive change. The task of this movement is to amplify their actions and voice globally.

This argument is connecting a generation in America, Europe, and Africa who are increasingly focused on tackling the root causes of gender and racial injustice. Poverty is Racist – that is true. This growing movement can build on other lessons we have learned from our campaigning.

Famous National and Global Political Action-Forcing Moments

ONE and RED have already used events such as World AIDS Day to shift money and policy to fight HIV around the world. More such action-forcing days are required for specific goals and targets. One big Global Goals Day for the world would help but not suffice. The goals cannot just be for policymaking elites in New York, DC, or London. Every country must take responsibility. We need a movement of Global Goal scorekeepers owning the agenda and holding local leadership accountable for their promises to their people. The public in every country must know about, own and help implement the goals, or at least a subcomponent such as girls' education or fighting corruption about which they personally feel most passionate. That requires informed entertainers across comedy, music, acting and sports to take their fans on a journey from apathy to awareness and action.

Helping makes us happier

We all share a yearning to belong, for life to have meaning, to be part of something bigger than ourselves. When we lack it, we become demoralized or depressed and withdraw or lash out. We are happiest for longer when helping others, or engaging in communal activities like choral singing or chanting in crowds at football stadiums. Populist politicians have manipulated these mass endorphins for short-term ends. We need to seize them for long-term progress through mass inspirational and informative seminars. TED summits, the Global Citizen Festivals and efforts like RED Nose Day, Live 8 or Agit8 are decent examples, but we need to go much further. At their best, U2 shows combine information, inspiration, and connections with a crowd. We need to be evangelical about key facts. We call our campaigners "Factivists" – fact and evidence based activists – to capture the spirit of this informed, inspired citizenry. As Bono once put it: "As a rock star, I have two instincts. I want to have some fun, and I want to change the world." This campaign must be an opportunity for people to be both effective, have fun, and meet others who share the goals. People need to be inspired, but they also want to be given precise practical actions they can take to make change happen.

The "Inside" - what policies we must press for and whom we must press

1. Focus the policy – especially on the poorest girls, women and most marginalized

The Global Goals are big, and there is some resistance to focus. Investing in the poorest girls and women at the grassroots is often the best way to lift up the whole community. Targeted social safety payments to marginalized citizens can transform their outlook and opportunities, by giving access to the basic needs of health, food, education, water and energy. We must ensure every marginalized adolescent girl and woman receives a digital and legal identity, connectivity and an online bank account into which targeted social safety payments can be made to help her access basic services. Such programs have proven highly effective in pilot programs. Now we must scale them to reach the most marginalized girls and women – and young men potentially at risk from extremist ideologies.

2. Find the money

There are four types of finance to fund this pro-poor program and accelerate progress towards the Global Goals. First, there is global public finance – development and humanitarian aid. The world will need much more if we are to sail towards safety over the next 15 years. There is misguided talk that the days of aid are over. It needs to increase if we are to achieve human security, even while other forms of finance increase. We can start by changing the name: think of smart aid as an investment in human security, a global insurance policy targeted at the world's most marginalized citizens with long term security benefits for all. In recent years, aid to the very poorest countries has actually gone down – a trend that must be aggressively reversed. The average Least Developed Country has only on average US$ 222 per person per year to spend on development and spends less than that on its poorest people. For the poorest people in the poorest countries, smart aid remains key.

Second, there is domestic public finance – funds raised by governments in taxes or debts to pay for development. Countries need to increase economic growth and tax revenues from their own economies. Capacity building for tax collecting authorities may not be an easy slogan on the streets, but it's one of the most important policies of all.

Third, there is private sector investment, ultimately the true game-changer. The global private sector is frightened of the world's poorest places for fear they won't make a profit or will be forced into corruption or rapid withdrawal because of conflict. But Unilever, SAB Miller, Diageo and the mobile phone companies represented by GSMA – who have fully endorsed the Global Goals – have shown how this can be done. More should follow suit. A focus by governments on fighting corruption and promoting the rule of law would encourage further responsible private sector investment. Patient capital in pensions and sovereign wealth funds must be incentivized to invest in the infrastructure of sustainable development, notably energy and transport.

3. Follow the money

Once we have focused on the right policies and found the funds to implement them, we need to be able to follow that money. We need a transparency and open data revolution so that citizens can make sure cash gets where it is needed. Progress will accelerate, and fewer will be left behind, when people, policymakers, and the media can see the money moving from taxes raised, funds invested, and aid allocated through open government budgets and procurement all the way to inspecting whether local governments delivered promised services. We also need to be able to follow the corrupt or questionable money when it tries to go underground. As the Panama Papers scandal underlines, there is a murky global underbelly of the financial system which needs to be opened up and reformed to reveal opaque centers and legal structures where corrupt leaders and violent extremists hide their finances.

One world declaration: the nine demandments

1. We demand everyone everywhere be treated equally because we are all members of one human family.

2. We demand access to basic opportunity for all – healthcare, education, nutrition, water, sanitation, infrastructure, finance, clean energy, connectivity, and basic social services – that enables us all to be healthy, happy and empowered to make our own unique creative contribution.

3. We demand political leaders at all levels are honest, open and direct about their failings and their successes. If they are not, we demand the right to access justice, hold them accountable and boot them out through free, fair and fairly financed elections.

4. We demand public and private institutions are open and honest about their funding and offer accessible decision-making through which citizens everywhere can "follow the money" and hold these institutions regularly accountable.

5. We demand advertising and information from the private sector and government which describe the true cost of products to people and planet.

6. We demand that all media are truly fair, factual and balanced, and we demand a global network of journalists with impeccable independent investigative journalistic standards to root out corruption as well as to tell good news of progress.

7. We demand the world's natural resources are sustainably managed for our future family's welfare as well as our own.

8. We demand that all local law enforcement and regional and global peacekeeping forces are properly funded and professionally managed to the highest ethical standards.

9. We demand everyone everywhere receive, read and react to the Universal Declaration of Human Rights and the Agenda 2030 of the new Global Goals for Sustainable Development.

So – that's one potential vision for a better safer sustainable world, which recognizes that poverty is sexist, there is a human security crisis, the solution is equality, and the time for action is now. What's yours? But please, let's not debate too much. Let's also get on with it, as time is short.

For data to be open and available, it also needs to exist. There's actually a data crisis in development policy as so many key facts are unknown. For example, a third of births and at least as many deaths and their causes are never registered. Most poverty data is a decade out of date.

The Global Goals risk being inherently top-down. We need to ensure they become bottom–up, with a citizen's Global Goals scorecard in Eva Tolage's hands, so she can monitor what's happening locally, and her whole generation can do the same, linked up globally. Mobile phone-based innovations are underway to enable just that, but we need to scale them up rapidly to hold the system accountable.

4. Who to target?

A few years ago, groups like ONE and our partners achieved great change by targeting a few leaders at summits such as the G7. Now we must also target leaders at the African Union, the G20 and global gatherings like the UN and IMF and World Bank meetings. Fifteen years ago this would have been impossible, but online organizing is possible as never before. We must also ensure the heads of global corporations, their boards, and institutional shareholders are influenced by praise or criticism and adopt the right policies. Influential figures in social media must be encouraged to lead this movement. Leaders of all faiths must be asked to return to the compassion and justice within their traditions. This movement must be unrelenting in demanding we all do better – while having a sense of fun and not becoming too self-righteous. Ultimately world leaders aren't really those people running countries. We must all be world leaders. Every citizen taking action locally is a leader. We need to start by targeting our own apathy.

One world, one family: we're all citizens of the Sahel now

The goals are massive and risk being meaningless. Something so big, so important, can start to lose definition. So we must not forget what is at stake. Just a few hundred Homo Sapiens sapiens survived about 100,000 years ago in what is now known as the Sahel. We sneaked through that window of fate and went on to populate the planet. What happened there then probably taught us much about how to survive since. What happens there now may do so again, but we must change our ways if we are to survive and thrive into the twenty-first century.

Bono recently wrote about a girl he met in Daadab refugee camp in Northern Kenya called Atong – which means "war" in Somalian. She was born in war, she lives as a refugee, and her homeland has been in religious and ethnic conflict all her life. More countries will suffer the same fate, expelling more refugees at risk of being attracted by more extremists' ideology, unless we act together now. With Eva and Atong we must now build a bigger stronger global movement for a better safer world, not just for them – but for us all.

Solving Energy Poverty and Adverting Climate Crises through an Off-grid Solar Electricity Revolution

By **Jacqueline Novogratz**

Under Jacqueline's leadership, Acumen has approved investments of more than US$ 101 million in 89 companies in Africa, Latin America and South Asia, all focused on delivering affordable agricultural inputs, education, energy, health care, housing and water to the poor. Prior to Acumen, Jacqueline founded and directed the Philanthropy Workshop and the Next Generation Leadership programs at the Rockefeller Foundation. She also co-founded Duterimbere, a micro-finance institution in Rwanda. She began her career in international banking with Chase Manhattan Bank. Jacqueline has been featured in Foreign Policy's list of Top 100 Global Thinkers and The Daily Beast's 25 Smartest People of the Decade. Jacqueline is the author of the best-selling memoir *The Blue Sweater: Bridging the Gap Between Rich and Poor in an Interconnected World*. She holds an MBA from Stanford and a BA in Economics/International Relations from the University of Virginia.

Energy poverty is an enormous challenge that we must address if we are to realize Global Goal #7. More than one billion people currently live without access to electricity. Changing this fact requires us to involve the entire energy ecosystem and combat the status quo within governments, the kerosene mafias and customers. However, the declining costs of solar energy and the ubiquity of mobile technology offer a unique opportunity to rise to this challenge. In her article, Jacqueline Novogratz argues that we can make no more important bet than building an off-grid energy ecosystem aimed at providing energy to those living in poverty without electricity.

In a world of growing interconnectedness, we are forced to face the stark inequality of other's divergent experiences – including the impact of climate change on the poor. Sustainable economic development and global peace mean not just the absence of violence but increasing opportunity and potential for humans to thrive. To realize Global Goal #7 and ensure universal access to affordable, reliable and modern energy services by 2030, the world can make no more important bet than on bringing off-grid solar electricity to the 1.2 billion people[1] on Earth currently living in darkness.

Imagine a world in which the rooftop of nearly every household in the developing world holds a small solar panel to provide not only light, but electricity to charge their phones, radios, TVs, and eventually, refrigerators, small appliances, and stoves. Even the lowest income households would have access to basic electricity, thus saving money otherwise spent on kerosene. Imagine a world in which households far from the grid can access clean, affordable electricity by turning their rooftops into energy generators. As households increase energy consumption, they earn and save more, thus contributing to a positive trajectory. Now, imagine micro-grids with smart meters linked to cell phones that utilize mobile payments; and new DC appliances, all of which could help households, enable small business creation, and encourage other increasingly productive uses of clean electricity.

In Sub-Saharan Africa alone, 621 million people are not currently connected to the existing power grid[2]. Despite US$ 31.5 billion already committed to grid extension through 2018[3], progress on reaching the poor thus far has been particularly slow, expensive[4] and reliant on non-renewables, including diesel and coal.

Daunting as this may seem, the precipitous drop in the cost of solar energy and the ubiquity of mobile technology on the continent present an enormous opportunity. Since 2009, photovoltaic solar module prices have dropped more than 75%[5], contributing to rapidly declining costs across the solar industry.

Our work at Acumen over the last decade has taught us that low-income customers will pay for products that are affordable and add value. d.light alone has brought solar products to more than 54 million customers and is currently on track to reach 100 million by 2020[6]. Companies like M-KOPA, Mobisol, and Off-Grid Electric are proving the growing demand and financial viability of pay-as-you-go in-home solar systems. These are just a handful of the successful innovations of the past few years, both in the technology and in the business models that bring such products and services to market. In the midst of these rapid changes, it is possible to see off-grid solar energy not simply as a bridge to the grid, but as a destination in itself.

However, the accelerated evolution of this sector has revealed a number of ways in which this energy ecosystem is broken. This affords a challenge and an opportunity to rethink the ways that we can support its successful maturation. The primary obstacle in is that governments are too focused on the historical solution – extending the existing grid – which is extremely expensive, and will likely take decades instead of years.

We have had some limited success in moving millions of people to the first rung of the energy ladder to solar lighting, all with a private sector approach. But the prospects of successfully scaling this model without involving the entire energy ecosystem are unclear. Large chunks of the value chain – mainly in marketing and distribution – remain missing or weak. There are too many small, mostly under-funded companies trying to do too much with too little capital.

Entrepreneurs building an off-grid energy ecosystem will have to combat an entrenched status quo in three areas: government, with a vested interest in extending the grid; diesel and kerosene mafias; and customers themselves, who know the ins and outs of working with biofuels every day. Fear of change is the greatest ally of the status quo, but intrepid entrepreneurs committed to leading the charge have an opportunity to offer an attractive alternative to the people who need it most.

The international community will need to leverage two trends – the falling cost of solar, and the advancements in mobile technology – to move distributed solar energy sharply beyond this inflection point. The falling cost of solar allows high-quality, affordable, and most importantly, scalable solutions to be made available to consumers as they move up the energy ladder. Mobile technology advances enable access to and engagement with those same consumers through metering, billing, and payments enabled by their existing mobile networks.

There are a number of ways to accelerate this new approach, but it is paramount to take a human-centered approach that recognizes the poor as customers instead of passive recipients of charity. Before we provide solutions and support demand, we must understand the energy needs of the poor, their purchasing power and how we can move them up the energy ladder and into the modern energy market.

Social enterprises are closest to these low-income customers and are driving innovation to find faster, more efficient solutions to provide the poor with new opportunities and the promise of a brighter future. But we need to bridge the funding gap by investing catalytic capital in this under-invested sector. That will require a mix of strategic grants and long-term investment capital. The more precious of the two is grant capital structured in a way that can leverage significant private investment.

To grow these companies, entrepreneurs committed to serving the market require a unique mix of early-stage start-up capital (financed by philanthropic-backed patient capital investors), working capital (which should at least in part be made available in local currencies with government guarantees, credit enhancements and other concessionary vehicles) and consumer financing. Guarantees should also be utilized as incentives for local banks to create working capital facilities in local currencies – something woefully absent

Solar industry growth has produced steadily falling prices

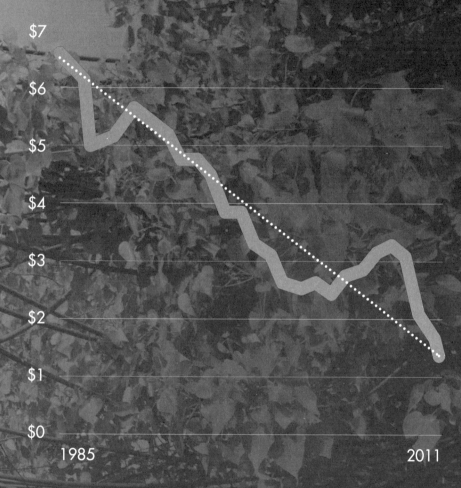

$7

$6

$5

$4

$3

$2

$1

$0

1985   2011

Module pricing trends 1985-2011

Source: Acumen via costofsolar.com

from the African energy sector, particularly in countries with significant devaluations of their currencies.

Specifically, grant funding is needed to create first-loss reserves to make bets on making the off-grid market more attractive to private investors. Grant capital is also important for technical assistance, both for management (building real talent in this nascent sector, especially at middle and senior levels) and for the R&D needed to bring better, lower-cost technologies (metering and batteries) to the market to help companies build upon their models and attract outside investment.

At the macro level, governments will also have a substantial role to play in ensuring an enabling environment for early-stage energy companies operating in developing markets. Reducing tariffs on imported components and guaranteeing bulk orders for solar products can facilitate more ambitious research and design while concessionary financing and discounts can lower prices even further.

This will not be easy. Igniting a solar revolution aimed at the poor will require innovative funds that invest in and support solutions across the energy ecosystem. Long-term investment funds combined with adequate technical assistance funding will enable a focused, accountable push not only to strengthen individual companies but to build solutions across the value chain – from marketing, financing and distribution to service/repair. Used correctly, these funds can create the models needed to show the world that off-grid solar solutions not only transform billions of lives but do so in ways that are cheaper, more efficient, faster and cleaner than by extending the traditional grids.

The success of the full off-grid solar ecosystem will provide energy access to large communities in a financially and environmentally sustainable way. In addition to the direct impact on the lives of millions of people, a fully functioning ecosystem will prove to governments and the market the value of this model for the future.

We have a chance to solve long-term energy poverty and avert a climate crisis. There is no better way than ensuring universal access to clean, affordable electricity. We don't have dignity unless all of us have dignity, and there's no better bet we can make than this.

---

1. International Energy Agency. http://www.iea.org/topics/energypoverty
2. International Energy Agency. http://www.iea.org/topics/energypoverty
3. White House, "Fact Sheet: Power Africa," July 25, 2015; and White House, "Fact Sheet: Powering Africa: Increasing Access to Power in Sub-Saharan Africa," August 5, 2014
4. Rural off-grid connections are projected to cost between US$ 1,300 – US$ 1,900 per household (Antonio Castellano, Adam Kendall, Mikhail Nikomarov, Tarryn Swemmer. Brighter Africa: The Growth Potential of the Sub-Saharan Electricity Sector, McKinsey & Company, February 2015, p.24)
5. International Renewable Energy Agency. Renewable Power Generations Costs in 2014, January 2015
6. http://www.dlight.com

Changing the World, one Childhood at a Time

By **Kailash Satyarthi**

Nobel Peace Laureate Kailash Satyarthi, Founder of Kailash Satyarthi Children's Foundation, is an advocate of children's rights. He and the grassroots movement founded by him, Bachpan Bachao Andolan, have liberated more than 85,000 children from exploitation and developed a successful model for their education and rehabilitation. He has been at the forefront of driving child-related agendas vis-á-vis the Global Goals. Mr. Satyarthi was the architect of the single largest civil society network for the most exploited children, the Global March Against Child Labor, which led to the adoption of ILO Convention 182 on the Worst Forms of Child Labor in 1999. He also serves as the Founding President of the Global Campaign for Education. In 2014, Mr. Satyarthi was jointly awarded the Nobel Peace Prize for the "struggle against the suppression of children and young people and for the right of all children to education."

Kailash Satyarthi believes children must be at the core of the Global Goals agenda. The argument is simple: to reach our common sustainable development vision, we need to engage youth and children as equal partners. This not only requires protecting children from violence and injustices, but also providing every child with the basic needs and tools to become her or his own change maker. To realize this, Mr. Satyarthi outlines a big bet built on three core pillars – strengthening the capacity of stakeholders in the child protection chain, training children and youth to be advocates of their own rights, and establishing a high-quality knowledge base capable of informing child policies across the globe.

I believe in the positive power of change. In addition, I know children and youth can lead the change the world needs, to end violence against all children. It is essential that we, adults, provide the right conditions, financing and frameworks for children and youth to realize their potential and overcome the conditions under which so many currently suffer.

With the support of various world leaders, I pressed for the addition of the abolishment of child labor, child slavery and violence against children in all forms to the Global Goals. Our collective efforts resulted in the inclusion of specific language in Sub Goal 8.7: "Take immediate and effective measures to eradicate forced labor, end modern slavery and human trafficking and secure the prohibition and elimination of the worst forms of child labor, including recruitment and use of child soldiers, and by 2025 end child labor in all its forms."

The violence inflicted by child labor is serious and is not limited to a child's physical, mental, spiritual, moral or social well-being. It subjects children to the worst form of humanity and a lifetime of vulnerability, exploitation and multiple forms of violence, hazardous conditions at work, acute hunger and illiteracy and denial of the basic freedom to exercise their rights. Currently, about 168 million children worldwide are serving in labor – almost 10% of the world's population between the ages of 5 and 17 – and around 5.5 million are in slavery. More than half of these child laborers, around 85 million, are involved in hazardous work. The magnitude of this issue requires the elimination of child labor to be given top priority and integrated into national and international development plans, policies, and programs.

Adding to the severe labor conditions, millions of children are continuously losing their childhoods in conflict-prone environments. In Syria, an entire generation is being deprived of their rights, and we have set the ground for worse outcomes in the future. UNICEF reports that 5.6 million children are living in dire situations and face poverty, displacement and violence. It breaks my heart to witness these increasing numbers.

There is also growing intolerance amongst youth and with the need to feel associated with a group, our children are more vulnerable than before. Unless harnessed and guided well, their energy and enthusiasm may turn into impatience, intolerance, and violence. This annihilation of childhood troubles me, and if it wasn't enough already, terrorists and insurgents have started abducting and employing children for their own vicious motives.

In response, we need to leverage the potential of our children who have regular access to food, water, shelter and schooling. They are hungry to make a difference and are looking for new avenues through which to deliver promises of a just and equitable future. The Global Goals need youth and children not just as stakeholders, but as equal partners for their realization.

Innovating beyond incremental improvements

As we embark on the path towards a more sustainable world within the next 15 years, we must ask ourselves: will rapid change enhance or diminish the extremes that make distinctions between our children based on class, color, nationality, financial state, and educational qualification?

We have to make a choice. Will governments, humanitarian organizations, partners in civil society and the private sector continue on the same path, recording incremental improvements in the situation of children but not closing the gaps? Or can we be bolder, trying unconventional approaches and looking for solutions in new places to accelerate progress towards a future in which our most vulnerable children can enjoy their rights?

There is in fact, no better state than vulnerability to be innovative. Innovation is an evolutionary process and to create a better future, we need to think more creatively with a committed focus on our children and youth. For all children to have an equal opportunity to realize their full potential, innovation must not only benefit those who can afford it but reach, meet the needs, and secure the rights of those who are the most marginalized and invisible.

My big bet for a better world is built on three equally important pillars:

Building capacity
We need to build capacity of stakeholders in the protection chain – children themselves, trade unions, teachers, the private sector and civil society groups along with international and regional organizations. This will help garner moral and physical support and enable us to secure financial resources.

The most imperative element is creating awareness and sparking political will to end violence against children in all forms. We need to reach all segments of society and compel them to prioritize children socially, economically and politically.

Government bodies, civil society networks, and concerned organizations need to study what has worked and develop robust, best-demonstrated practices. Capacity-building curricula for individuals and institutions should be developed and adapted to local contexts and languages in order to ensure impact. Specifically, the following practices should be undertaken:

- Creation of standard training modules and methodologies to train the police, judiciary and civil society organizations.
- Development of child rights curricula units for children and for judicial academies.

Educating leaders
To truly ensure a sustainable long-term solution for youth, we need to create a generation of leaders, not followers. Globally minded children and youth need to be trained to advocate for their rights. As they mature into adults and become

leaders, their empathy and compassion will translate into an unprecedented level of global and sustained action and vigilance. This is the world's best chance for bringing about an end to violence against children.

We need to enable, empower and engage children and youth by educating them about their rights and providing them with a platform to exercise those rights. Effective advocacy cannot be achieved without the support, voice and leadership of our children. They are the embodiment of the cause and we need them to lead the movement.

Through the Kailash Satyarthi Children's Foundation, I intend to build a large-scale global advocacy campaign to instill a sense of global citizenship and engagement among children and youth. Our outreach will focus on increased child participation at all levels and encourage children to advocate for their own rights as well as those of other children – thus building social equity and urging systematic inclusion through the democratization of knowledge and institutional reform.

We will build a movement centered around engaging youth and children to become aware, sensitized and compassionate about the rights of children and act urgently, uniformly and collectively to eliminate exploitation and violence against children around the globe.

Establishing the knowledge base
To underpin all global efforts related to improved opportunity for children and youth, it is vital to strengthen knowledge accumulation and mobilization. With available, accessible and high-quality data, we can influence government policy makers to create the necessary infrastructure to ensure our children's

rights. Public awareness of the legal instruments for the protection of children against labor, trafficking, slavery and violence has to be increased along with knowledge, capacity building and sensitization on the issue.

We need to address policy gaps by conducting data-driven, evidence-based research, documentation of findings and best practice in child protection, health, and education.

The key to prevention and more effective treatment is to re-examine or recast policies and programs around the needs of the child. Currently, they are fragmented across child protection, education, labor and health departments. Some programs, such as school meals, link education, and basic nutrition/health, but greater overall coordination is needed.

Our foundation has set goals to identify and conduct research on key issues related to violence against children to identify and prioritize key gaps in systems, frameworks, policies and investments and will test solutions through pilot programs. We will create a database as an international reference point for knowledge on child rights with evidence of impact in achieving a child-friendly world.

The honesty, innocence and moral strength of a child is difficult to match. If given a chance to advocate for themselves, children's humanity will cut across inequalities, categories of class and caste, economic disparity and political borders and strive towards finding solutions with a human soul. Violence is not only manifested externally, but it has its roots in the multiple facades of structural inequality. To achieve peace and spread compassion, we need the sanctity of children – clean and untarnished by adult prejudice – to decide our fates.

We need to believe in the strength and ability of youth to be change makers. Even more, we need to make them

168
million children
worldwide are
serving in labor

85
million children
are involved in
hazardous work

57
million children of
primary school age
worldwide are out of
school

Sources: ILO, Marking Progress Against Child Labor, 2013 and UN, MDG Progress Report, 2015

aware of the power they possess, and the capacity to think of themselves not as powerless but central to the solution. In the struggle against slavery, I have witnessed children take charge and lead their families, other children, villages and societies out of the darkness innumerable times.

The story of Payal is a testimony to such exemplary leadership and strength. In 2012, my organization adopted Hinsla village in Rajasthan as a Bal Mitra Gram (BMG) – a child-friendly village where children attend school and are free from all forms of exploitation. Central to this idea is the concept of child engagement in matters involving the community. Children's rights are protected with the active involvement of the villagers, the Bal Panchayat (Children's Council), the village council and the local administration.

Payal, along with other children in Hinsla, began protesting against the evils of child marriage and ghunghatpratha – an age-old tradition which requires women to cover their faces with a veil at all times. That not only reinforces men's supremacy over women but helps perpetuate the system of patriarchy prevalent in North India.

Payal carried the entire weight of this rudimentary school of thought on her little shoulders. She decided it was time for change. Instead of succumbing to family pressure to marry young, she went to school and continued to fight against the social injustice.

Her perseverance serves as an inspiration to all girls living in similar circumstances. Her commitment brought her to the forefront of the fight. She was elected as the Head of the Children's Parliament (Bal Panchayat) in Hinsla, and her continued efforts led her to be a jury member for the International Children's Peace Prize, aged just thirteen.

It is in these moments that one realizes the power of participation and youth. Their voices are critical to this work, and their efforts are unmatched in our fight. Each figure has a face, and every data point is a lost childhood. We have ignored their cry for far too long. But not any longer. Let us not neglect the needs of our children. Let us enable them to take over the world.

A Thousand-Day Plan to Level the Playing Field for All Children

By **Luis Alberto Moreno**

Luis Alberto Moreno has been the President of Inter-American Development Bank since October 1, 2005. Mr. Moreno chairs the Board of Executive Directors of the Inter-American Investment Corporation (IIC) and the Donors' Committee of the Multilateral Investment Fund (MIF), both institutions of the IDB Group. Before joining the IDB, Mr. Moreno served as Colombia's Ambassador to the United States for seven years. In his country, he had a distinguished career in the public and private sectors. Mr. Moreno served as Minister of Economic Development, President of the Instituto de Fomento Industrial, and manager of social investment policies, including the housing strategy for low-income families. In the private sector, he advised major Colombian companies and foreign investors and was executive producer of a leading television news program.

Recent research suggests that investing in nutrition, vaccination, and cognitive stimulation during the first three years of a child's life could be the most cost-effective ways to reduce inequality.

Over the last two decades, many low- and middle-income countries have made remarkable progress in closing the nutrition and health gaps between the richest and poorest children. And in many ways, Latin American and Caribbean countries have been ahead of the curve. They demonstrated great commitment to advancing health equity and, as a result, several indicators – such as infant mortality – have improved dramatically.

Nevertheless, health and cognitive indicators among the region's poorest children are still worrisome. Significant disparities in nutrition and vaccination persist, particularly in rural areas. Due to insufficient investment in early childhood, many children also start school with disadvantages in their cognitive development.

This already troubling picture could worsen in the coming years. Like other developing regions, Latin America and the Caribbean are undergoing a nutrition transition. People are switching from traditional cereal- and fiber-based diets to eating more processed foods filled with sugar and unhealthy fats. Being overweight is becoming as much of a problem as undernutrition. In fact, both can coexist in the same family or even in the same individual, a situation that University of California at Berkeley professor Lia Haskin Fernald has defined as the nutritional paradox. Today, this growing public health problem affects the most vulnerable children in the region: those born in poor and indigenous communities. In Guatemala, 50% of children under five have chronic malnutrition while 50% of mothers are overweight.

Beyond these significant issues, there is yet another critical gap that has been traditionally overlooked but is related to the region's high levels of inequality: the cognitive gap. While children in Latin America are now healthier and more likely to attend pre-school, those from poor households lag far behind their peers from more affluent families in learning, particularly in the areas of language and cognition.

New research traces the cognition gap back to the frequency and quality of the interactions that children have with adults, whether at home, in day care or in pre-school. For example, early age vocabulary richness is a good predictor of school success. But one study in five Latin American countries found that, at age 5, children of mothers with low education levels recognized fewer than half the words recognized by the children of better-educated mothers. Likewise, it concluded that children who spend hours with poorly trained staff at day-care facilities would be better off if the adults they come into contact with were coached on how to properly interact with and stimulate children.

Some countries have made laudable efforts to increase spending in the first 5 years of life. Coverage of services such as day care, pre-school or home visiting programs has expanded dramatically in different countries. However, in order to ensure that investments in early childhood have the desired impact, governments will have to change the focus from expanding coverage to improving the quality of services.

Governments should also strive for achieving greater equity in spending across age groups. An Inter-American Development Bank study, The Early Years (2015), shows that Latin American and Caribbean countries spend three times more on educating children between the ages of six and 11 than they do for children aged five and under. Investments for

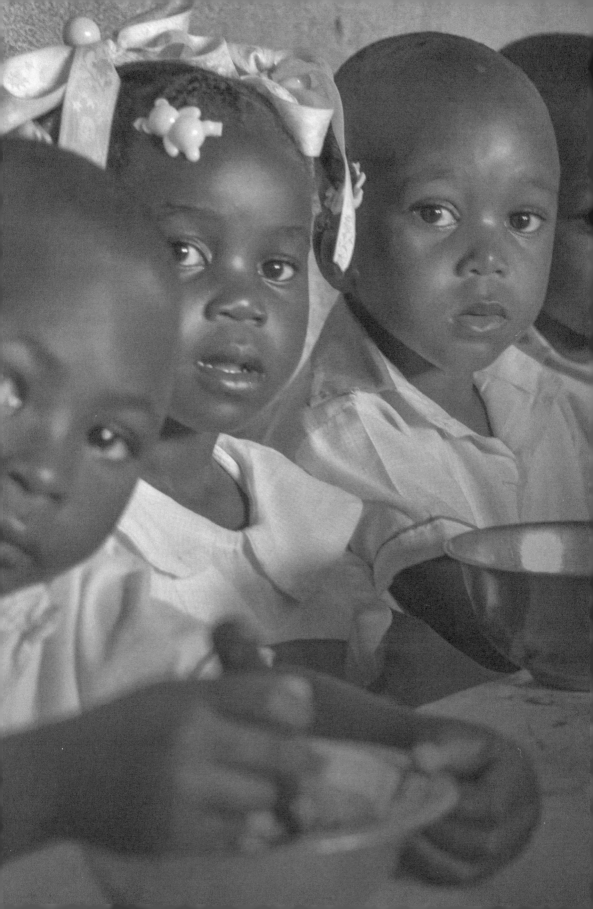

5.9

million children
under 5 died in 2015

83%

of deaths of children under age five
are caused by infectious, neonatal or
nutritional conditions

Source: WHO, 2015: http://www.who.int/gho/child_health/mortality/mortality_under_
five/en

child development have focused on older children rather than the younger ones, who benefit the most from health, nutrition and development interventions. Evidence has shown that intervening at a younger age has impacts on productivity and health later in life. The only way that children in our region will reach their growth and development potential is to increase investment directed to younger children.

A good example of how such investments pay off can be found in Jamaica. As part of a pilot research program, community health workers visited the homes of malnourished children for an hour every week over the course of two years. The visitors, who were adequately trained in the delivery of a psycho-social stimulation curriculum, brought age-appropriate toys for the kids and advice on child-rearing for the parents. Researchers tracked the outcomes of the program for more than one generation. The results are astounding.

Children who received home visits grew to become adults who earned 25% more than their peers in other families. On average, they had higher IQs and were less likely to suffer from depression or to commit crimes.

Even more remarkable is the fact that the home visits – a relatively inexpensive intervention – were ten times more effective than day care in improving cognition. Despite such evidence, many governments still view building more day care centers as a priority rather than investing in high-quality parenting programs.

At a time of economic slowdown in most developing countries, it is critical that governments focus their spending on what really works. I believe there is enough scientific evidence to push for a comprehensive, first one thousand days of life care package to ensure that every child has a fair shot at becoming a healthy, stable and productive adult.

From Argentina to Zambia, there are three things that governments in the developing world should prioritize in their spending, and that could be made free and universal for all children.

First, countries need to guarantee access to better basic healthcare, particularly for the poor. Setting goals with regard to reducing inequities in investments between the rich and the poor is key to improving indicators, for example by achieving vaccination rates in rural areas equivalent to those in urban populations. Governments will benefit from the use of health information systems to pinpoint the communities where they need to focus efforts, monitor progress and improve performance.

Second, in order to achieve the 2025 target of reducing stunting in children under 5 by 40%, countries should set themselves the goal of ensuring adequate nutrition for all children. Government efforts should focus on improving infant feeding and care practices, as well as access to safe water and health services in the key period from conception to the first 24 months of life.

Third, governments need to rethink their early childhood development policies and services. A high-quality program would combine effective home visits and parenting programs with well-equipped day-care centers staffed with properly trained caregivers. The goal would be to ensure that, whether at home or in day-care, every child has access to adults who can provide adequate care and stimulation during this critical period in life.

With the right mix of investments, targeting, training, and the availability of both Early Childhood Centers and home visit programs, we can radically improve all children's ability to learn and thrive later in life.

Shifting Power to Protect People and Planet

By **Annie Leonard** *&* **Daniel Mittler**

Annie Leonard is the Executive Director of Greenpeace USA and the author of The Story of Stuff, an online film that has been watched over 40 million times around the world. The film grew into The Story of Stuff Project, which works to empower people around the globe to fight for a more sustainable and just future. In 2010, Simon & Schuster published Leonard's New York Times bestselling book, The Story of Stuff.

Daniel Mittler is the Political Director of Greenpeace International. Based in Berlin, he leads Greenpeace's global team advising the organization on political and corporate strategies. He has led Greenpeace delegations to many global negotiations and writes on NGO strategy, climate politics, and corporate accountability. His writings can be found at greendaniel.blogspot.com.

If we are to realize the Global Goals, we have to change the way we govern our planet. We need a new distribution of power, in which world leaders from all sectors are accountable to all citizens instead of the top 1%. Governments must not only create but also implement regulations that secure the public good. Daniel Mittler and Annie Leonard focus on three global policy shifts: to give social and environmental governance bodies real power; to ensure the primacy of politics over business; and to control the financial industry.

With the Global Goals, the world has agreed on an important to-do list for humanity, a vision to end poverty by 2030, to turn the tide on soaring levels of inequality and to accelerate the transition to a world run on safe, renewable energy. However, these goals – like too many agreed by government summits before – will not be met unless the next 15 years sees a fundamental shift in the distribution of power. Nothing less will be required to deliver prosperity for all while staying within the ecological limits nature sets us.

Today, political and economic power is held by a small fraction of people – many of whom have strong ties to the very industries that threaten sustainability. Unless we shift the balance so that our political and business leaders are accountable to all citizens instead of the 1%, we are stymied in our ability to advance real solutions. Our big bet is that this can be done. Governments must put regulations in place that secure the public good and give the institutions implementing these regulations the tools to do so. We know this is both possible and necessary. A redistribution of political and economic power is a precondition for achieving Global Goals.

The work to get us there has already started. Across the world, citizens are joining together and raising their voices for a fair and sustainable future. For now, rather than responding, governments all too often turn their backs, while rolling out a red carpet for corporate donors. Global economic players gaining from the current destructive status quo have captured global politics, obstructing real solutions that move us closer to meeting the Global Goals. The result is that the world has already exceeded four of seven "planetary boundaries", inequality is rising and in many places, the space for civil society to act is shrinking.

But the ground is shifting as citizen power grows. Over the last year, the Keystone XL pipeline was cancelled following pressure from a diverse coalition of citizens, farmers, indigenous communities and others; Shell had to withdraw from the Alaskan Arctic in the face of people – from grannies to investors to kayakers – opposing drilling for more oil than our climate can handle; China's use of coal has gone into decline, not least because people are unwilling to put up with the unsafe air that it makes them breathe; and President Obama recently halted coal leases on US public lands. No sector has changed as much in the last 15 years as energy. Already twice as many Americans are employed in the solar power industry as in coal mining. And the revolution towards clean, renewable energy will accelerate. Clean, renewable energy is getting bigger, better and cheaper every day. Renewables are the most economical solution for new power capacity in an ever-increasing number of countries. There is now 15 times more installed solar power and three times more wind power in the world than in 2007. On a global level, more clean power capacity is being installed than coal, oil, and gas put together. Solar power, for one, is growing faster than even we at Greenpeace predicted.

This encourages us. But to enable a fair and just development path, we need more fundamental changes than just switching from fossil fuels to renewable sources. Governments must agree on rules that secure the public good. They must empower public institutions to deliver and enforce these rules. That means changing some fundamentals in the way we govern our planet, including how our global institutions and regulations work. We propose three key global policy shifts:

- Giving real power to global bodies dealing with social welfare and environmental protection.
- Ending corporate trade deals and ensuring the primacy of politics over business.
- Regulating the financial industry.

1. Give social and environmental governance bodies teeth!
Institutions are created by humans, and if governments want to create powerful bodies, they can. Today, those who protect the status quo are the most powerful, while those protecting people and their rights are often impotent. The World Trade Organization (WTO) can impose punitive fines on countries that break its rules. It is a place where support for renewable energy is under attack. The United States recently got the WTO to strike down local content rules in India's renewables program. Giving preference to local producers is against the WTO rule that all producers should be treated "equally". In an unequal world, this formal insistence on equality only serves to reinforce the dominance of the already powerful.

Because the WTO keeps ruling in favor of the status quo and the powerful – and has teeth to enforce its rules – it is having a chilling effect on progressive politics, making governments less likely to take decisive action, such as making polluters pay for climate pollution.

In contrast, environmental and sustainable development governance is not effective. The many institutions are not coordinated and lack adequate powers. The UN Environment Programme (UNEP) can only plead, coach and build capacity. Environmental and social bodies should also be able to impose sanctions and fines. UNEP needs to be turned into a global authority for the environment, with greatly enhanced implementation, compliance, and enforcement mechanisms. Other environmental treaties must also be strengthened. It should be clear that if governments break the agreements they have signed up for – such as Canada did when it refused to implement the Kyoto Protocol on climate protection – there will be real consequences.

2. Ensuring that politics rule

Global institutions need to change, but economics also has to be brought back under control. Governments face a choice. They can further trade agreements like the Trans-Pacific Partnership (TPP) or the Transatlantic Trade and Investment Partnership (TTIP) and give corporations more powers to undermine and undo policies in the public and planet's interest. They will allow corporations to sue governments acting in the public interest. That will result in more absurd law suits, such as those by Swedish energy utility Vattenfall, suing Germany to be compensated for that country's sovereign democratic decision to phase out nuclear power; or TransCanada, suing

American taxpayers because President Obama rejected the Keystone XL pipeline in the interests of humanity.

Alternatively they can choose a different path, one centered on shared power and the public good. They can open up, become more transparent and democratic and share power with citizens. A complete social and environmental review of the global trade system is long overdue. The negative impacts of the current system need to be revealed and a new system built, centered around a sharing economy.

Also, governments can put us on the right track by ending the global impunity of the corporate sector. Corporate accountability and liability should extend to all impacts on people and the environment around the world. If corporations cause harm, they need to incur a real cost. A binding global instrument that ensures full liability for any social or environmental damage must be a high priority if we are to achieve human-centered development by 2030. Such an agreement is not as utopian as it may sound. At the World Summit on Sustainable Development in 2002, governments agreed that there needed to be global rules for global businesses. If governments are serious about the 2030 Agenda, it is time they acted on this promise.

At the national level, we need to reawaken democracy and ensure that politics sets the rules for business, not vice versa. In the United States, for example, this implies immediate measures to reduce the influence of corporate money in elections, candidates for office publicly refusing fossil fuel money and protecting voter's rights.

3. Control financial markets
Sustainability and justice can simply not become a reality in a world in which short-term bets by financial markets prevail.

Strong controls of financial markets are an essential first step for governance for people and planet. New fiscal instruments such as a financial transaction tax need to be agreed globally to slow harmful speculation and deliver much-needed finance for development and environmental protection.

These are just a few of the many approaches we know could shift the balance of power away from corporations which would mortgage our future for short-term gain. We know these measures can work and deliver better welfare for people as well as help ensure we do not exceed global ecological limits. So why, if people and planet will benefit, are these steps not being taken today? Why is there any risk of us losing our bet?

From local to global: end capture of politics by polluters

That's where we have to return to the question of power. With the increase in extreme weather events like Hurricane Sandy in 2012, the majority of Americans now support effective climate action. The fossil fuel industry, however, dominates US politics, thwarting effective action. And it is not just in the US. Big business has captured too many governments, in both North and South. From Capitol Hill to Caracas, Brasilia, Ankara and New Delhi, the oil, coal and gas industries still rule. Even common sense measures such as cutting fossil fuel subsidies are unable to progress. Now governments have agreed at the Paris climate conference, to strive to limit global warming to 1.5 degrees Celsius compared to pre-industrial levels, it is

These goals – like too many agreed by government summits before – will not be met unless the next 15 years sees a fundamental shift in the distribution of power.

simply absurd that public money is being spent to make the climate problem worse. This contradiction is especially vexing in countries that face real constraints on their public finances. That governments still spend some US$ 452 billion every year on subsidizing fossil fuel production in the G20 alone can only be explained by governments prioritizing the wellbeing of Exxon and Koch Industries more than their citizens.

A movement of movements to change direction

Political action and activism in the next 15 years must focus on changing existing power relations. In order to deliver governance for people and planet, we are determined to build on the victories people have already scored. We will work to build a movement powerful enough to force governments to act in the public interest. To do so, we are determined to build alliances between grassroot initiatives and global organizations and to make the argument for fundamental change as much on the street as in the corridors of power. We know it can be done, because we are doing it.

It was diverse alliances ranging from conservative farmers along the route of the pipeline as well as global investors realizing the ages of fossil fuels is ending; it was local activists and indigenous peoples as well as global environmental organizations such as ourselves that stopped the Keystone XL pipeline, for example.

Robert Hunter, one of the founders of Greenpeace, once observed that "big change looks impossible when you start, and inevitable when you finish." We realize our bet that governments will govern our people, and the planet will seem impossible and idealistic to many. We know that the global trend has been away from effective rules towards deregulation and consequent environmental destruction. But just as (formal) civil rights were delivered, and Apartheid ended, we believe that governance for people and planet will one day be achieved. With your help, we can make this dream come true in time for the world to deliver on the Global Goals by 2030. As Nelson Mandela observed, "it always seems impossible, until it's done."

Adopting Inclusive Business Models to Address Income Inequality and Unemployment

By **James Mwangi**

Dr. James Mwangi is world-renowned for his contribution to financial inclusion in his role as the Group Managing Director and CEO of Equity Bank – one of Africa's leading banks, specializing in inclusive business models. He is the Chairman of Kenya's Vision 2030 Delivery Board, charged with ensuring Kenya becomes a middle-income country by 2030. In 2012, he was named the Ernst & Young World Entrepreneur of the Year, the Forbes Africa Person of the Year and the African Investor African Business Leader of the Year in 2013. He was ranked among the *Financial Times* top 50 Emerging Markets Business Leader in 2010.

In 2015, the World Economic Forum identified rising income inequality as the most significant trend and ranked unemployment second. These worrisome trends constitute the most significant challenges in connection with the realization of the Global Goals. In response, James Mwangi makes a big bet on the widespread adoption of inclusive business models and a stronger and more determined engagement of the private sector to support them. Inclusive business models democratize economic opportunities for the poor by integrating them into markets as producers and consumers in a single global ecosystem. Current models, however, often do not take into account the real potential of serving the poor and pursuing sustainable impact beyond mere profits. Dr. Mwangi argues that if done correctly, inclusive business models can aid us all in creating shared prosperity across different segments of the population as envisioned by the Global Goals.

The World Bank has set a highly ambitious poverty target (defined as those living below US$ 1.90 a day) at 3% of the world's population by 2030. In 2012, the number of people classified as extremely poor stood at 896 million (equivalent to 12.7% of the world's population), compared with 1.95 billion people in 1990, and 1.99 billion people in 1981[1]. While the decrease in overall poverty is a remarkable achievement, the current numbers are still worrisome. The poverty eradication targets towards 2030 will not only require a dramatic acceleration of current efforts to expand GDP in a way that creates jobs and reduces poverty, but also new measures and approaches. As a significant share of global poverty eradication in the past 15 years has been led by China, lifting the next billion people out of poverty will require new thinking and adaptation of new models.

High income inequality dampens GDP growth rates, and the fact that many countries are characterized by a widening gap between the rich and the poor is a cause of great concern. As we move into the post-Millennium Development Goals (MDG) era, we are still facing enormous challenges with income inequality, unemployment, and poverty. In order to meet these challenges effectively, we ought to shift the current aid-based development approach to a more empowering and private sector-led development paradigm based on partnerships and the use of inclusive business models. These models are designed to serve the unbanked and under-banked populations by treating them as vital actors in national economies and allowing them to enter the economic system. The models target low-income markets to achieve scale through a high volume of small transactions.

Defining inclusive business models:

"Inclusive business models are commercially viable and replicable business models that include low-income consumers, retailers, suppliers, or distributors in core operations. By adopting the models, companies build the capacity of low-income businesses and entrepreneurs; increase access to finance for businesses and consumers; create or adapt products to meet local needs and requirements; and develop innovative distribution approaches to hard-to-reach communities.[2]"

The private sector plays a vital role. It contributes to wealth and employment creation, innovation and enhanced productivity, and is increasingly being recognized as a lever for socio-economic progress. Governments, especially in cash-strapped developing countries, are rarely in a position to provide much more than basic and often incomplete social amenities for their citizens. So far, many governments have not been sufficiently successful in creating an enabling environment in which the private sector can thrive. As such, the ingenuity and agility of the private sector constitutes a significant and often untapped resource for progress in society. The private sector has the potential to create the majority of jobs needed for countries to prosper.

Models of inclusion

Numerous challenges still exist when it comes to doing business with the poor. A majority of the poor population participate in the informal economy and often fail to be recognized by the formal businesses sector despite being potential consumers and producers. Such realities call for a unique approach to serving the poor, which is my big bet – adaptive inclusive business models.

The uniqueness of inclusive business models lies in how they manage to integrate the poor into market value chains as producers on the supply side (employees, suppliers, distributors) or consumers on the demand side. These models shift the paradigm by going beyond seeing the poor as non-actors in business, seeing them as potential partners rather than simply those who can only consume philanthropy and corporate social responsibility. These models perceive people, despite their economic status, as critical success factors in businesses performance, and not just a means to generate profits. These models bring innovation and enormous social impact by empowering those people who were previously powerless in the face of the formal economy.

Businesses are increasingly including the poor, but significant challenges remain. We need to expand access to finance, reach these new producers and consumers through the right infrastructure (branches, agent and mobile phone banking) and provide the information needed on the resources of the poor. This is vital in order to create sustainable and inclusive businesses which can help alleviate the challenges of poverty, unemployment and income inequalities that we still face today.

While the term 'Inclusive Business Models' may be a relatively recent catchphrase in the development lexicon, Equity Bank has, right from its inception, recognized the incredible latent power that lies at the bottom of the pyramid and made it a business to unlock this power for mutual benefit and development. When we started operations in 1984, the poor in Kenya and many African countries could not access formal financial services. The industry was steeped with barriers to entry that deliberately excluded the poor: minimum opening amounts, minimum account balances, monthly ledger fees, restrictions on the value of transactions, and introductory letter requirements, among others. We made a strategic decision to remove these barriers to enable low-income customers to access financial services. The poor were invited as partners and were served with dignity.

This was a complete switch in how banks served poor people in Kenya. Before that, poor people never thought banks were for them, and banks treated poor people in a way that reinforced the idea that banking was the preserve of the rich.

There are 411 million mobile money accounts globally

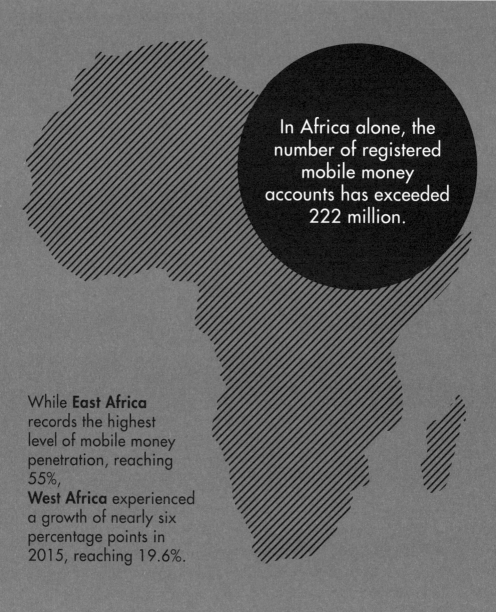

In Africa alone, the number of registered mobile money accounts has exceeded 222 million.

While **East Africa** records the highest level of mobile money penetration, reaching 55%, **West Africa** experienced a growth of nearly six percentage points in 2015, reaching 19.6%.

Source: GSMA, State of the Industry Report – Mobile Money, 2015

Numbers of registered and active (90-day) customer accounts, by region*

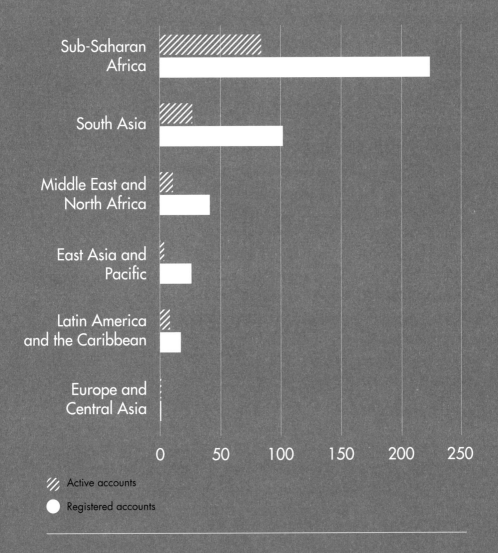

Active accounts

Registered accounts

*Mobile connections linked to a mobile money account. 'Active' is measured on a 90-day basis

Today, Equity Bank serves over 10 million individuals and business clients in Kenya, Uganda, Tanzania, Rwanda, South Sudan, and the Democratic Republic of Congo. As the concept of inclusive business models is being implemented in practice, both producers and consumers are empowered. Concretely, efforts in innovating non-traditional banking channels such as the agency model and Equitel, a recently launched mobile virtual network operator which provides secure and cost-friendly mobile banking, create gains on both sides. As a business, the bank reduces its fixed costs as it moves away from bricks-and-mortar structures. The result is an increase in the number of transactions while members gain jobs and profits as bank agents, and convenience and minimized transaction costs as clients.

Inclusive business models are raising turnover and wages, creating jobs, providing social and economic products, and building creative innovations for a better society. Today, Equity Bank is a banking conglomerate with one of the largest customer bases on the African continent, but other banks are becoming more receptive to this poor market segment and the idea of inclusion. We welcome this and support any attempt to further open up the economy to the bottom of the pyramid.

Leveraging best practice

To combat extreme poverty and reduce the number of extremely poor people to less than 3% by 2030, we need to democratize economic opportunities by investing in inclusive businesses that maximize both economic and social benefits.

Inclusive business models offer ways to do this and create win-win opportunities that allow private sector players to grow their bottom lines while having social impact and solving pressing global concerns.

To effectively deliver on the Global Goals and ensure increased empowerment and inclusion of the poor in national and global economies, governments and policymakers should provide a conducive environment and social amenities, and the private sector should work closely with governments in tackling the challenges of our time. Our efforts must be inclusive to ensure that we do not exclude any segments of society.

---

1. World Bank, Poverty overview, 2015, http://www.worldbank.org/en/topic/poverty
2. International Finance Corporation. 'Inclusive Business at IFC May 2015

Thought Girls' Education Was Big Before? It's Bigger Now. Here's How.

Count, Consult And Connect: A Path To Transformation

By **Craig Silverstein** *&* **Mary Obelnicki**

Craig Silverstein and Mary Obelnicki are the founders of Echidna Giving, which works to get more girls into better schools, to live better lives. As a Stanford graduate student, Craig saw a world-changing idea and left academia for the garage that became Google. Fourteen years later, another world-changing idea propelled him to the Khan Academy, where he is Dean of Infrastructure. Mary earned her engineering degrees at MIT. Her fusion of analytical thinking and social change led her to the on-line community organizing of Big Tent, a Coro Fellowship in public affairs, and her philanthropic work with Craig. Both remain engineers, with a belief in the power of data and rigorous analysis to make ideas reality.

For 25 years, girls' education has been a big bet in the global South. Those delivering education programs have gone way beyond desks and uniforms. They've had to address all aspects of girls' lives: nutrition, reproductive health, safety, community norms and economic prospects. This work has uncovered an even bigger bet: rather than this one sector doing everything for girls, how about all sectors do their one thing for girls? Today, we have 25 years of expertise to show us how. Any sector – health, agriculture, energy – can start by weaving three proven practices into their existing work: count, consult and connect girls. The result will be more girls whose education brings benefits across their families, communities and nations – and more systems that support all girls and women. In other words, more societies that work for everyone.

Let's rewind the clock to one of the biggest bets of the last century. In the early 1990s, evidence started to accumulate that investing in girls' education could break intergenerational cycles of poverty. The following decades saw girls' education programs, studies, conferences, articles, movies. Today, it's one of the few development approaches that anyone outside of the field has heard of – due to Malala's story, Boko Haram, #bringbackourgirls, and the like.

But after 25 years, we are not even close to delivering on the promise. There are more girls in primary school today. But are they learning? In South Asia, almost half of all 4th-6th graders can't read a newspaper, and more than half can't add or subtract. These numbers look slightly better in most of sub-Saharan Africa, but not much. Furthermore, the true payoff of education comes when girls graduate from secondary school with real skills. In sub-Saharan Africa today, barely a third of girls are secondary school graduates. We have some work to do.

But there has been progress in shining a bright light on how to make systems work for girls. Our big bet for the 21st century is that **the global community acts on those lessons**. If that happens, the payoff will extend far beyond girls' education. Here's how.

The evidence is in: the ripple effect is real

Even if girls' education has yet to deliver full returns, it's not a bet anymore but a sure thing. Decades of evidence demonstrate that when educated girls grow up, they have smaller, wealthier, healthier families. They're more likely to survive childbirth, as are their infants: millions of boys and girls are alive today thanks to their mothers' early education. These kids are more likely to go to school themselves, leading to gains in wages, agricultural productivity, and overall GDP. There's even emerging evidence that education can help build immunity to religious radicalization, an urgent global need. These are huge results from relatively small investments. Right now, we've seen these gains mostly in East Asia and Latin America. How are we going to make these changes happen everywhere?

What works? Think nutrition, cash subsidies, and real job opportunities

In 2015, Gene Sperling and Rebecca Winthrop published a seminal survey of what works in girls' education, drawing from thousands of programs over the last 35 years[1]. The bottom line: girls have a unique ability to end cycles of poverty, but poverty still has the upper hand. It forces families into hard choices, like prioritizing their sons' health and education over their daughters'. It fuels violence inside communities, limiting girls' ability to even travel to and from school. It leads to early marriage and subsequent school drop-out.

So NGOs with successful education programs go way beyond schools, uniforms and books. Where scarce food goes to the boys, these programs ensure girls have adequate nutrition. Where inadequate infrastructure requires girls to be water-carriers and care-givers, programs subsidize families for the loss of their daughters' labor. Where expectations for girls stop with marriage, NGOs persuade communities that an educated daughter can make as much as – if not more than – her brothers. To successfully educate all students, these providers tackle poverty-driven barriers that disproportionately affect girls.

But the education sector alone is simply not big enough to lift the weight of poverty. That load is too heavy to be borne by the efforts of any sector, and the education sector receives only a tiny slice of overall development funding. Rather than one sector doing all things for girls, how about all sectors do their one thing for girls?

A new big bet: it's not one lever, it's many!

Take Bangladesh. Over the last 30 years, multiple sectors have redirected their efforts to work better for girls: The education system reduced families' material hardships, the health system improved mothers' and girls' health, the economic development sector built schools where girls could easily access them, and the private sector increased demand for skilled workers. In 2011, 80% of girls completed primary school, up from 66% in 2005, and 65% completed secondary school, up from 50% in 1998. By 2015, teen pregnancy dropped, more mothers, babies, and children had survived, and the country's GDP had grown 6-6.5%. A different group of NGOs tried the same approach in Burkina Faso and achieved similar results.

So how can people in other sectors learn how to do their one thing for girls? There's no need to wait for all sectors to show up. Today, 25 years of girl expertise have defined actions that any organization in any sector can take to benefit girls, their families, and their communities now – without dropping everything else they're doing. Call them quick starts. There are three of them: count girls, consult with girls, and connect girls.

If you don't count girls, girls don't count

If every program, policy, or approach to international development simply counted girls – that is, disaggregated its data by sex and age – the impact would be extraordinary. Act on those numbers, and the impact is game-changing.

Just because an effort could include girls doesn't mean it does, and counting is the simplest way to find out. Girl advocates have been rightly demanding this for decades. If policymakers or program designers don't know whether girls are receiving benefits, how will they know how to respond? Even if they can't respond right away, the raw data reveals a story that everyone needs to know, given the ripple effect that girls can have.

Echidna Giving's partner Educate! teaches workforce readiness and leadership in the Ugandan school system. They disaggregated their data by sex and found many of their top graduates in Kampala were female. As they expanded to rural areas, their data showed female participation dropping. This led them to count rural female staff and mentors. No surprise, there was a correlation. Had they not counted, they would have had an effective entrepreneurial program, but mostly for boys. Instead, they could take steps to ensure girl-friendly features such as female mentors were included when their program went rural.

Consult with the experts: girls themselves

Once girls are counted, it's clear who's missing – and it's clear who can tell you why. Women and girls are geniuses in meeting their own challenges, and the organizations that harness their smarts see results. The methods are nothing fancy. They ask girls what they need, listen to what they say and co-design solutions. They put women and girls in leadership positions – then make sure those leaders have a real role in decision-making.

Liberia's Economic Empowerment for Adolescent Girls and Young Women (EPAG) project involved girls in its planning, and discovered that transportation and scheduling were huge issues. The solutions were straightforward: offer training close to girls' homes, with two sessions a day. Sure, others might have raised these issues, but would they have been able to prioritize them? Would they have come up with the most effective solutions? By involving girls, those things took care of themselves.

Girls and young women want to help each other: connect them!

When they pursue a future that differs from the one pursued by their mothers or grandmothers, girls face enormous cultural pressure and even violent opposition. (There's a reason why the Taliban shot Malala.) They need a safe place where aspirations are cheered rather than challenged, where vital information comes from a trusted source (another girl or woman) and where role models offer proof of new possibilities. Imagine a woman truck driver going to an all-women community meeting. Just by showing up, she provides an example to girls and an industry connection to young women. Call it critical mass, the network effect, or just people supporting each other. Giving girls and young women the space, time, and skills to create relationships is one of the most sensible methods for creating change – one connection at a time.

In Guatemala, the Population Council's Abriendo Oportunidades fosters girl connections within the indigenous

Girls are in school but not learning

**Percentage of 4th, 5th and 6th grade
students who are <u>not</u> proficient**

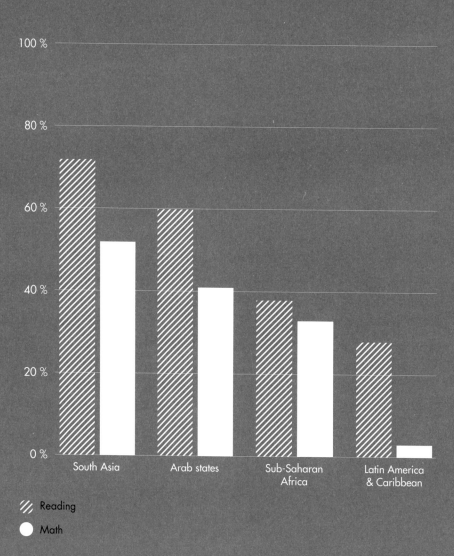

100 %

80 %

60 %

40 %

20 %

0 %

South Asia   Arab states   Sub-Saharan
Africa   Latin America
& Caribbean

/// Reading

⬤ Math

Data Drawn From Sperling & Winthrop, 2015 And UNESCO's World Inequality Database
On Education.

The promise of girls' education has been proven over the last 25 years

GIRLS' EDUCATION IMPROVES:

MATERNAL & CHILD HEALTH

- Drove 50% drop in maternal mortality from 1990 – 2010
- Drove 50% decrease in child mortality from 1970 – 2009, saving 4.2 million lives
- An extra year of education cuts child mortality by 5% – 10%
- Educated, sub-Saharan women have 2.8 fewer children

CHILDREN'S EDUCATION & WELLBEING

- Kids with educated moms have 4.1 more years of schooling
- Educated moms are linked with childhood immunizations
- 26% fewer children would suffer from stunting, if all girls were educated

ECONOMIC GROWTH

- Drove 25% economic growth, across 30 OECD countries
- Each additional year of schooling boosts GDP by 5% – 12%
- Each additional year of schooling increases future wages 10%

HEALTHIER AND WEALTHIER COMMUNITIES, STRONGER NATIONS.

Data source: Graphic summarizes impact data presented in Sperling & Winthrop, 2015.

Mayan community. They've learned that, with support and structure, a girl's inherent desire to connect can change her life. The program creates safe spaces for girls, connects them to mentors, and trains older girls to become safe-space leaders and mentors to younger girls. Each of these connections is an avenue for life skills and financial training. The model works: compared to national averages, these girls remain childless, single, and in school longer, with nearly half of them hired for paid jobs.

What it all adds up to

Most of these examples come from organizations that focus on girls to begin with. Where are the examples of programs that just want to make sure their efforts are working equally well for girls and boys, men and women? So far, it's girl pioneers who have designed and measured these practices.

Today, we can close that gap. We can have public transportation systems that simply count girls, to find out if they can safely travel to school or work or friends; children's book publishers that make sure half their characters are women; energy agencies that find more efficient ways to keep family homes warm and lit by consulting with girls – the primary fuel-collectors – who gain free time for study as a result; factory owners who connect young women so they can show each other the ropes; and public health organizations that measure girls' education where they do their work, because they know that's a direct reflection of how well they are supporting girls in general.

Through simply counting, consulting and connecting girls, we can move the promise of girls' education to the next level – faster and further, across nations and regions.

But that's not the biggest bet. There's an even bigger payoff when all sectors do their one thing for girls. These steps can ultimately do away with the notion of "girls' education" as its own sector altogether. Because the truth is there's really no such thing. There are just education systems that either work for girls and women – or do not. Health systems that work for girls and women – or do not. Economic systems that work for girls and women – or do not.

When we place this big bet on systems that truly work for all people, it's not just the education of girls that will finally pay off, but the fullest potential of girls and women across all facets of their lives. And if there's a bigger bet than that, we'd like to see it.

---

1. What Works in Girls' Education: Evidence for the World's Best Investment (Brookings Institution Press, 2015) builds upon the foundations of a 2004 survey of the same name, coauthored with girls' education champion and expert Barbara Herz

Cultivating Equality in the Food System

By **Danielle Nierenberg**

Danielle Nierenberg is President of Food Tank and an expert on sustainable agriculture and food issues. She has written extensively on gender and population, the spread of factory farming in the developing world, and innovations in sustainable agriculture. Danielle has traveled to 60 plus countries across sub-Saharan Africa, Asia, and Latin America interviewing hundreds of farmers, researchers, scientists, activists, policy-makers, and other stakeholders, collecting their thoughts about what is working on the ground to help alleviate hunger, obesity and poverty while also protecting the environment. Danielle has an M.S. in Agriculture, Food, and Environment from the Tufts University Friedman School of Nutrition Science and Policy and spent two years volunteering for the Peace Corps in the Dominican Rep.

Women are still routinely ignored and discriminated against in the food system. Investing in women farmers and entrepreneurs not only constitutes a route towards greater equality but will also help to increase food production in a sustainable way. This article presents the idea that a combination of traditional knowledge and indigenous practices combined with modern technologies holds the potential to make farming more efficient, less labor-intensive, and more profitable. In the end, it has the potential to lift millions of people out of hunger and food insecurity. Women farmers need support from international research and development agencies; and policymakers in the developing world should invest in education and new technologies. While the path towards our sustainability vision surely is very difficult, there is no doubt it should be marked by more coordination and conversation with women farmers.

Imagine a world where 30 years from now, farmers produce 50% more food than today; child malnutrition is practically non-existent; more nutrient-dense foods have replaced those which are highly processed; post-harvest losses are prevented with innovative, low-cost technologies; girls see a future on the farm and beyond; and climate change is something we no longer deny but which is being mitigated by farmers through sustainable agriculture. And we didn't get there with a new, costly, silver-bullet technology, but something both very simple and revolutionary: investing in women farmers and entrepreneurs.

Women make up more than half the world's population and nearly half of its farmers, but their contributions are almost universally ignored. Female farmers are at least 43% of the global agricultural labor force, and in some parts of sub-Saharan Africa the proportion is as high as 80%. This invisible sisterhood accounts for a large share of the world's food producers, yet these working women are often denied access to education, refused support by banking and financial institutions, and ignored by extension agents and research organizations. They are still routinely discriminated against simply because they are women.

Many of the world's women farmers are actively preserving biodiversity, improving nutrient density for their families, and finding ways to prevent post-harvest losses, preserve crops and create value-added products. By working to strengthen the voice of girls and women in agriculture through information and communication technologies, they are also cultivating the next generation of agricultural leaders. With the new Global Goals in place, it is time to realize that we ignore women and girls in the food system at our own peril.

Caretakers of biodiversity and nutrient density

While men typically produce cash or commodity crops that need to be processed into something else, women grow most of the vegetables and fruits and raise the livestock that nourishes families. In Cote d'Ivoire (Ivory Coast), the conflict that erupted in 2002 after a coup d'etat had a huge impact on agriculture in the northern part of the country. According to Slow Food International, women farmers – the majority of the agricultural workforce – were especially hard hit by a decrease in incomes. Yields and incomes decreased and many children stopped going to school because of the violence. For those who still attended, the meals served were often of poor nutritional quality.

Mariam Ouattara, the President of Chigata Fettes et Development (Women and Development), an NGO in N'Ganon village, responded by launching Slow Food Chigata to grow organic food and to cook meals for the children. She believes obesity and other health problems have been the result of the large-scale import of food sold from elsewhere in Africa and Europe. The chief and the elders, who remember traditional foods, "have jumped on the project" to help educate students, teachers and community members about "how to eat." They hope that through the children, they can change how parents cook and eat with "trickle up education." Ouattara says: "Once children eat, it's easier for them to become better students."

In India, the Self Employed Women's Association is helping increase nutrient density and empower women farmers and consumers. The organization – which has more than one million members and is one of the largest unions in the world – grows organic rice, lentils, spices and other products, and markets them under its own label. It works with women vendors in urban areas, helping them to market and sell to other low-income women in slums.

But it can't be only NGOs taking the lead on improving nutrient density. Women farmers need support from international research and development agencies to ensure that they have the ability and the resources to grow fruits, vegetables, and nutritious grains. The UN Food and

Agriculture Organization should invest in pilot projects in sub-Saharan Africa, Asia, and Latin America that help train women researchers and extension agents who can work with farmers to protect and improve access to indigenous crops.

Transforming food

Over the last 50 years, one consequence of the Green Revolution is that agricultural production has narrowed to the production of raw commodities including corn, soy, and wheat, with less focus on more nutritious foods such as millet, sorghum, perennial grains, and vegetables. Funding for research on cereals and grains is now roughly 13 times that for fruit and vegetables. While the poor in developing nations get most of their calories from starchy crops, there has been very little funding to understand what makes these staples palatable.

But vegetables are not only nutritious, they also add taste and variety to staples. Unfortunately, tomatoes, okra, and leafy greens including amaranth, spiderwiki and other vegetables indigenous to Africa, Asia, and Latin America tend to have a short shelf life. Most are only available for part of the year. During the "hungry" season before the rains, rural communities have few ingredients available to add flavor to the staples on which they depend.

At the AVRDC – the World Vegetable Center office outside Bamako in Mali – researchers and scientists are working with farmers to develop preservation techniques to make vegetables available year-round and transform them in the ways women want. Okra powder, for example, is commonly used in Mali for sauces, while powdered tomato products are not because women prefer fresh tomatoes for cooking. In India and the Gambia, women dry mangoes and other fruit with abundant but short growing seasons. The dried fruit can be sold to families all year round through local stores or to schools, providing an important source of Vitamin A.

According to the UN Food and Agriculture Organization (FAO), the International Water Management Institute (IWMI) and the Stockholm International Water Institute (SIWI), up to half of food in Africa is wasted before it ever reaches the dinner table, and at least one third is wasted globally. That makes it more important than ever to find ways to preserve and transform food. While most public-private partnerships in agriculture have been between large-scale, multi-national agribusiness companies and governments, there is an opportunity for food companies and retailers to work more closely with farmers and policymakers in developing countries.

Combining high and low technologies

The combination of traditional knowledge and indigenous practices combined with modern technologies is helping make farming more efficient, less labor-intensive and more profitable. In Niger, a group of 50 women farmers partnered with the International Center for Agriculture in the Semi-Arid Tropics to establish a communal garden using solar drip irrigation to grow vegetables, fruit trees, and other crops. They learned not only how to install and maintain the drip lines, but also to produce compost and other soil-building techniques. That has allowed them to increase production to feed themselves and increase their incomes five-fold with sales in the nearby capital, Niamey.

Throughout sub-Saharan Africa, Asia and Latin America, farmers are using technology to gather information about weather and markets, conduct banking and financial transactions, and communicate with farmers in nearby communities and even other countries. Cell phones are particularly important for women farmers because they can help erase gender barriers. Women can gain information that typically would not be shared by a male extension agent or agro-dealer. SMS is allowing women to buy inputs and receive payment without ever having to go to a bank.

Cuts to agricultural extension programs often mean there are just a few agents available to serve tens of thousands of farmers. But technology can help fill the gap. The Africa Rice Centre is designing and disseminating educational videos on agricultural techniques such as seed preparation. Farm Radio International is taking advantage of radio's popularity throughout sub-Saharan Africa with shows about improved composting methods and organic fertilizer to help farmers repair degraded soil, increase harvests, and improve incomes.

Governments need to find ways to make rural areas more exciting, intellectually stimulating places for young women and men alike. They need access to information and communication to see agriculture as something they want to do, not that they feel forced to do. Policymakers in the developing world have a responsibility to invest in education centers and wireless technologies, and subsidize cell phones for farmers so that they have access not only to technical information but also to one another.

On average, women comprise 43% of the agricultural labor force in developing countries, but they lack essential productive resources. If women had the same access to productive means as men, they could increase yields on their farms by 20–30%.

Female share of economically active population in agriculture (%)

20.9%

Latin America and the Caribbean

42.6%*

Asia

48.5%

Africa

52%**

Oceania**

Source: FAO, The State of Food and Agriculture, 2010-2011
Note: *Asia excluding Japan; ** Oceania excluding Australia and New Zealand

Growing sustainability

——

Sustainability in agriculture is not just a fad or a catch phrase. It nurtures a food system that does not lurch from crisis to crisis. It happens when techniques for surviving drought years developed by women in sub-Saharan Africa are shared with their peers in Asia, Latin America and even the United States who are also struggling with water scarcity.

The path to sustainability is not always clear. However, there is no doubt it will be led by coordination and conversation with women. According to the UN Food and Agriculture Organization, if women farmers had the same access as men to resources – of land, credit, education, extension services – they could increase food production by 20-30% and lift as many as 150 million people out of hunger and food insecurity. It needs to expand research to highlight the economic value of women farmers as well as their contributions to environmental and social sustainability. We also need farmers, policymakers, NGOs, research institutions and funders to recognize that science is our servant, not our master. Enabling technology such as cell phones should be subsidized for women.

Also, the UN Food and Agriculture Organization needs to expand its research to highlight the economic value of women farmers as well as their contributions to environmental and social sustainability. Women's work producing and preparing food needs to be quantified so that their contributions are valued.

Governments throughout the developing world also need to invest in establishing extension services specifically for women farmers. Creating training centers for female extension workers and establishing women-to-women networks of information sharing will allow women to get the access to resources and practices they need to improve nutrient density, prevent food loss, and increase incomes.

As Professor Olivier De Schutter, the former UN Rapporteur on the Right to Food has pointed out, women deserve equality in all parts of their lives, not just in agriculture. Let's be smarter and give them the recognition, value, and support they need to nourish both people and the planet.

Integration and Universality: Game Changers for Impact of the Global Goals

By **Amina J. Mohammed**

Amina J. Mohammed was a central player in the SDG process, serving as the Special Adviser to UN Secretary-General Ban Ki-moon on post-2015 development planning and structuring the overall framework for collaboration with respect to the development and ultimately the agreement on the Global Goals. She previously served as Founder and CEO of the Center for Development Policy Solutions and as an Adjunct Professor for the Master's in Development Practice program at Columbia University. She was the Senior Special Assistant to the President of Nigeria on the Millennium Development Goals. Ms. Mohammed was appointed Honorary Minister of the Environment by President Buhari when he swore in his Cabinet on November 11, 2015.

To successfully implement the Global Goals, we need to recognize universality, integration, and sustainability. Only by understanding that the Goals are meant for everyone – for all nations, all people and the entire planet – will we ensure that we reach our target for 2030. In this article, Amina J. Mohammed makes a big bet for integration and collaboration between sectors, countries and worlds, specifically focused on leveraging digital and mobile technologies for empowerment, ownership and success of the 2030 Agenda.

In the past, the world has managed to do amazing things when working in collaboration, lifting perspectives above narrow individual or national interests, and enacting important changes even when the challenges seemed at first to be impossible. Since 1990, there has been an incredible anti-poverty movement lifting more than 1 billion people out of extreme poverty, providing increased access to education and healthcare and improving the supply of food, water, and energy for millions of the world's most vulnerable. While these accomplishments are impressive and the Millennium Development Goals (MDG) took us far, we still have a long way to go. Now we have to finish the job. This will take another amazing push. My belief is that the 2030 Agenda will meet the objectives.

The new goals are ambitious and complex, and require substantial funding and effort from all partners to be realized. The context is different. It is not just about cutting the burden in half. It's about finally resolving some of the most daunting problems we face. To end poverty. To end hunger. To achieve prosperity for all. To take climate action and reduce the effects of climate change. This is no easy task. Eight hundred thirty-six million still live in extreme poverty. Seven hundred ninety-five million are undernourished globally. Also, only half of working-age women participate in the labor force, while three quarters of working-age men do[1].

The global goals framework - universality and integration

The Global Goals framework entails a novel approach to development. When we speak of sustainable development, it implies including social, economic and environmental considerations. While holism and synergy have always been buzzwords of development, they take center stage in the 2030 Agenda. The 17 Global Goals are not competing. They are interrelated, embracing the complexities and context of the current and emerging challenges.

In my view, the concepts of universality and integration are at the core of this paradigm shift. And they hold the key to successfully realizing our common Global Goals.

By universality, I do not mean sameness or uniformity. Universality does not imply "one size fits all" solutions. It simply means that the Global Goals apply to all. That all people have the right to live a life in dignity. That we leave no one behind. Countries will identify their own priorities while preserving the integrated and rights-based nature of the universal framework. Universality means uniqueness and flexibility, as contradictory as this might sound. There is no doubt that the MDGs have been an extremely powerful tool for achieving a shared development vision, but progress has been uneven across goals, regions, nations and even within countries. Making the Global Goals felt everywhere by everyone is critical.

I propose considering the 2030 Agenda in a cohesive manner, in all countries and for all people, mobilizing the participation of all actors. Integration means building partnerships, combining the strength of many actors and cutting across geographies with coherent efforts. I believe we need to see integration in three areas to tackle the root causes of our many challenges today.

A three-step integration of the 2030 agenda

First, we need integration between sectors. The leadership of governments, citizens, civil society, social movements, business, parliamentarians and local authorities will be necessary to ensure that we develop lasting horizontal partnerships to carry the 2030 Agenda forward. Integration between public institutions and private companies is especially critical. Not only do we need to collaborate and combine knowledge and economic resources when working on explicit projects, but we also need much closer alignment on basic issues: How do we work to improve accountability? How do we make sure that governments and private companies share the knowledge needed in specific cases? How do we enter into partnerships of trust and confidence? Visions and strategies of public institutions and companies would benefit from each other, if inspired by and aligned with the Global Goals. We have already seen examples of such collaboration. In my home region of West Africa, the African Cocoa Initiative is a public-private partnership in which government institutions in Ghana, Côte d'Ivoire, Cameroon, and Nigeria join forces with the World Cocoa Foundation, cocoa industry members, the Sustainable Trade Initiative and USAID to improve productivity within the industry. The initiative is an example of how to integrate different sectors on core development issues. Building public-private models to support effective and sustainable production and enhance food security has huge potential and captures the spirit of the Global Goals. It is certainly not easy to have different partners come together, but the potential is too enormous not to try[2].

Secondly, we need integration between countries. Success with the Global Goals will require concrete innovative policies and technological solutions between countries. It is the coherence and alignment of countries' policy frameworks, plans and financing strategies that will make a difference. One hundred ninety-three countries have pledged to deliver to people, planet, prosperity, peace, and partnerships, hopefully paving the way towards a sustainable future. Our 17 goals constitute a very explicit to-do list for governments across the world, providing a burning platform for close cooperation between countries. They define specific roles and responsibilities to respond to the different conflicts and capabilities of each country.

Thirdly – and this may be less straightforward – we need integration between worlds. By this, I mean the real and the virtual worlds. Whether in urban hotspots or distant rural areas, computers, mobile devices, and internet access are becoming common tools. Linking virtual technology to real-life challenges creates a platform for innovation in development. It also provides the fuel to ensure we drive the data revolution to ensure no one is left behind.

In 2015, 95% of the world's population was covered by a mobile cellular signal. The number of mobile subscriptions has skyrocketed to more than 7 billion. Internet penetration has grown from just over 6% of the world's population in 2000 to 43% in 2015 with 3.2 billion people linked to the Internet[3]. These basic facts highlight enormous potential.

Imagine, for instance, an online or SMS-enabled platform providing easy access to data, knowledge or technology on health care, finance or transport. This is already happening in many areas. In transport, ICT solutions can make transport easier and quicker, allowing people to work and socialize instead of waiting in line for buses. South African start-up WhereIsMyTransport (WIMT) has developed an online platform for urban transportation in emerging regions around the globe. Based on live data, WIMT connects commuters and operators for efficient journeys. This is both sustainable and scalable. In health, mobile technology also has tremendous potential. The promotion of health campaigns, gathering of data and improving maternal health by reducing the distance between women and health clinics are just a few of the many opportunities offered by eHealth. In my home country of Nigeria, we have seen SMS and printer technology used to allow local health facilities to receive and print HIV-test results from laboratories without computers and Internet access. In Mozambique, SMS reminders and educational messages have been sent to HIV positive people in order to improve treatment and prevent further transmission[4]. In agriculture, mobile technology may be a real game-changer, providing farmers

In my view, embracing universality and integration through digital platforms is essential if we are to deliver on the Global Goals. Imagine governments, private companies, research institutions and foundations from all over the world supporting technological capacity, information and financial resources to form and sustain open source platforms. Not only would that make existing platforms smarter and more efficient, it would also create and sustain new and powerful partnerships for development that result in new ideas, innovations and initiatives for the benefit of those in need.

with new agricultural techniques and useful information on commodity prices and weather conditions. This increases access to financial services and microfinance, enhances the link between buyers and sellers of agricultural products, and improves management of distribution networks[5]. In the short term, mobile technology in agriculture will help put food on tables in rural areas of developing countries. In the end, easy access to this type of information is crucial in mitigating the effects of climate change and managing population growth. The Ghanaian social enterprise Farmerline is already using ICT to communicate weather conditions, market prices, farming practices and financial tips[6]. It reaches more than 5,000 smallholder farmers in Ghana and more than 200,000 via partnerships in other West African countries. In Zambia, Rent-To-Own is riding the digital sharing economy wave by matching rural micro-entrepreneurs with productive assets such as hammer mills and irrigation pumps[7]. In many places across the world, environmental decision-making is being improved by new technology. For instance, the USAID and NASA initiative SERVIR[8] is a satellite-based flood forecasting and warning system that helps manage climate change risks in developing countries. These initiatives are impressive in themselves, but they are also scalable and applicable in many countries and industries.

In my view, embracing universality and integration through digital platforms is essential if we are to deliver on the Global Goals. Imagine governments, private companies, research institutions and foundations from all over the world supporting technological capacity, information and financial resources to form and sustain open source platforms. Not only would that make existing platforms smarter and more efficient, but it would also create and sustain new and powerful partnerships for development that result in new ideas, innovations and initiatives for the benefit of those in need. It also provides a huge opportunity to improve governance, strengthen institutions and ensure results in people's lives while protecting the planet.

We need to scale up innovations that have succeeded in the past and to test new promising initiatives. Many investments in technology and building partnerships were made during the MDGs. Now successes need to be expanded at scale with robust partnerships across constituencies and countries to achieve the development targets.

---

1. MDG Progress Report, 2015
2. World Cocoa Foundation. The WCF African Cocoa Initiative.
http://www.worldcocoafoundation.org/wcf-african-cocoa-initiative/
3. MDG Progress Report, 2015
4. WHO. Mobile health: Transforming the face of health service delivery in the African Region, 2015
5. In a study commisioned by Vodaphone, Accenture identified 12 ways in which agriculture could benefit significantly from Mobile Technology
6. Farmerline.org. http://farmerline.org/tag/ghana/
7. Rent-To-Own. http://rtoafrica.com/about-us/
8. Servir Overview. http://www.nasa.gov/mission_pages/servir/overview.html

Your World Aspiration

By **Olafur Eliasson**

Danish-Icelandic artist Olafur Eliasson (born 1967) works with a wide range of media, including installation, painting, sculpture, photography, and film. Since 1997, his critically acclaimed solo shows have appeared in major museums around the world. Eliasson's projects in public spaces include The New York City Waterfalls in 2008, and Ice Watch, shown in Copenhagen in 2014 and Paris in 2015. Established in 1995, his Berlin studio today houses about ninety craftsmen, technicians, architects, archivists, administrators, and cooks. Together with engineer Frederik Ottesen, Eliasson founded the social business Little Sun in 2012. This global project produces and distributes the Little Sun solar lamp for use in off-grid communities and spreads awareness about the need to expand access to sustainable energy to all.

Olafur Eliasson has a very clear message: art can motivate people to act by confronting them with concrete experiences and clear images. Often, we feel untouched when confronted by seemingly insurmountable challenges such as climate change and conflict. Art, however, when done right, has the potential to touch, move and motivate individuals and groups of people to take action even when it seems difficult. As such, a successful artwork builds a community around it – locally or even globally. Pursuing this line of thought, Olafur Eliasson outlines how art can empower people and provides two fascinating examples from his own portfolio to emphasize this very point.

Rather than a bet on a single technological invention, idea, or product to improve the world, my best bet for a better world is a bet on in the cumulative aspirational power that is expressed by all people on this planet through art and culture.

Participation in culture is a fundamental right, as outlined in Article 27 of the Universal Declaration of Human Rights. I propose that we take this right and all its implications seriously. This means not only ensuring the right to participate in culture, but also actively supporting culture and its practitioners, expanding access to it, and inviting more people to engage in its production and discussion.

This also means cultivating a broader trust in things that are unquantifiable, things that cannot be subsumed by market economies or made suitable for distribution through the hegemonic culture industry. It entails having confidence in the power of abstraction and in things which, broadly speaking, cannot be easily formulated in words – ideas and feelings that defy quick formulation and digestion. It is crucial to believe in the power of culture and the arts because these fields can reach people emotionally. They express our common aspirations and inspire our active involvement in the world.

Linking knowledge and feeling

A lot can be said about the importance of producing and expanding access to knowledge. The book you are holding in your hands, for example, is also engaged in the admirable task of increasing knowledge. Less can be said about how and why some data motivate us to act, and other data leave us feeling disconnected. This is because it is not enough just to give access to data. Data alone will rarely motivate change.

In fact, the opposite seems to be true: there is a disconnect between what people know and how they feel, and this translates into a lack of motivation and aspiration to connect to and improve the world. It is certainly important to present the data behind key issues facing the world today, but linking knowledge and feeling is necessary to mobilize responsible action.

One of the great challenges today is that we often feel untouched by major problems in the world; we do not recognize that we are part of a global community, a global we. This is where I think art and culture can play a unique role. Art is engaged on a daily basis with creating experiences that touch, move, and motivate people. Most of us know the feeling of being touched by a poem or a book, being moved by a piece of music or a work of art. Often when we are touched, we become aware of an abstract feeling that is already inside us – something we may recognize and even identify with but have not yet verbalized or understood entirely. Art can be about getting you to treasure unvoiced dreams or to wake up if you are dreaming too much. It can be provocative or critical, or it can offer you a much-needed moment of reflection.

Turning feeling into action

Art and culture can motivate people to act by confronting them with concrete experiences and abstract thoughts. Similarly, by pushing the limits of the possible, it can encourage people to form, express, and work towards their dreams and aspirations. It shows that the world can be changed by their actions, and that reality is relative. Through the bottom-up exchange that is central to the culture we co-produce our common values and aspirations for a better world.

Moreover, culture offers us a space in which disagreement and conflict are not considered solely negative; they are rather essential ingredients in experiencing art and culture together. An arts festival offers more potential contact, more inclusion, more conflict management than a political gathering, conference, or summit, where the lines of contention are more clearly defined; it brings together people from various backgrounds and hosts more progressive thinkers than any other gathering today. This space could be a great source of inspiration for politics and an antidote to populism and the demonization of other cultures and worldviews.

For me, art is about having an experience that is both shared and individual. We may disagree about the nature of an aesthetic experience, but fundamentally, the artwork connects us; we experience it together. A successful artwork builds a community around it – locally or globally – without doing so at the expense of others; it creates an inclusive environment where disagreeing is not only allowed but essential. We have to seek a language that allows for both being singular – me – and plural – us.

Touching ice and holding hands with the sun

An example of what I believe art can achieve is reflected by my project Ice Watch. Together with geologist Minik Rosing, I first organized Ice Watch in Copenhagen in 2014 to mark the publication of the UN IPCC's Fifth Assessment Report on Climate Change. We harvested twelve large blocks of ice from a fjord outside Nuuk, Greenland, and brought them to Copenhagen, where they were arranged in clock formation and left to melt in City Hall Square. Everyone could come to the square to touch the ice and experience for themselves the effects of global warming. In December 2015, on the occasion of COP21, we again displayed twelve blocks of ice in public space, this time in the Place du Panthéon in Paris. The work offers a concrete experience of climate change by bringing the melting glaciers home to the people who have the power to combat global warming. It's a physical wake-up call. Ice Watch confronts people with a radically concrete reality, which for most of them has only ever been an abstract topic that they

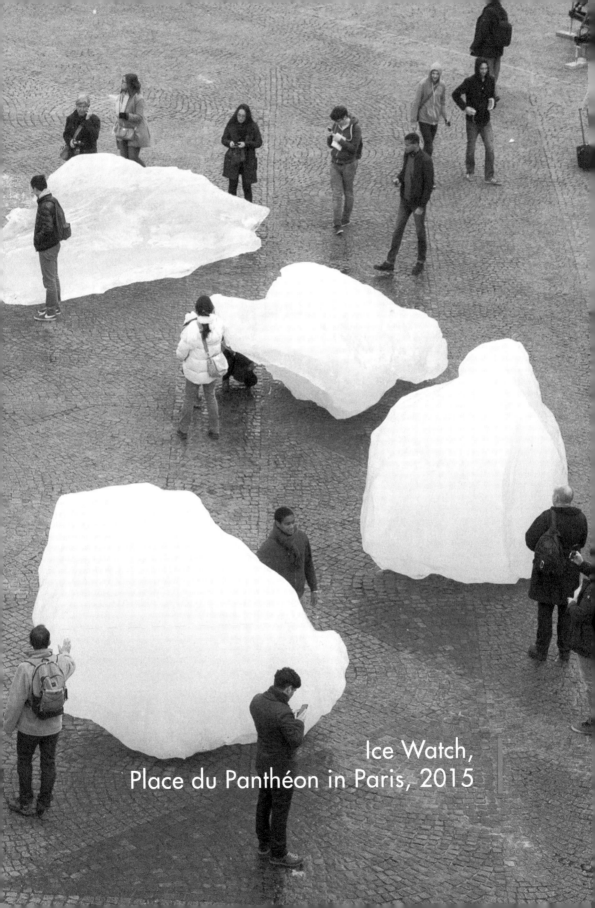

Ice Watch,
Place du Panthéon in Paris, 2015

have read about. It makes them physically feel the melting ice with their bodies rather than just intellectually, and this direct experience, I believe, can motivate them to take real action.

Another project I have been working on for some time now also triggers a feeling in order to motivate action: in 2012, I set up the social business Little Sun together with engineer Frederik Ottesen. Our aim is to promote solar energy for all. Little Sun reflects our belief that one of the keys to combating climate change lies in moving from simply consuming our limited resources to sharing and creating new sources of energy. The future must be energy positive. On a practical level, Little Sun responds to the need to develop sustainable, renewable energy by producing and distributing affordable solar-powered lamps, with a focus on regions of the world that do not have predictable access to electricity. But while Little Sun offers a practical solution to the problem of unequal energy distribution, it also creates an emotional bond to the discussion. Little Sun is about the self-esteem gained from feeling you have resources and are powerful. It takes something that belongs to all of us – the sun – and makes it available to each of us. It's not just about having access to energy; it's about being strong. It gives you the feeling of being empowered. With Little Sun, you are able to tap into the energy of the sun, to power up with solar energy. This feeling of having power is something everyone desires, and it is something everyone can identify with. Participating in Little Sun brings together people all around the world in a community based on a feeling.

The global we

As an artist, I believe that we need broader support for bottom-up creation and art practices everywhere. Our best bet for a better world – for a world in which people feel that their actions have meaning – is to empower people's sense of identity and interconnectedness through art and culture. This is the basis for real change. Art is the energy that inspires solidarity and community – a global we. By supporting art and culture, we support our ability to be motivated and to motivate.

For more insights on Big Bets for
a Better World, check out the
Big Bet Initiative webpage.

BIGBETINITIATIVE.COM